MANAGING
FOR THE MASTER

Other Books by G. Edward Reid

Authored Books
Almost Home
Battle of the Spirits
Even at the Door
It's Your Money! Isn't It?
Ready or Not, Here He Comes
Sunday's Coming!

Edited Books
Faith and Finance

MANAGING
FOR THE MASTER
G. Edward Reid

Pacific Press®
Publishing Association
Nampa, Idaho | www.pacificpress.com

Cover design and resources from Lars Justinen

The author assumes full responsibility for the accuracy of all facts and quotations as cited in this book.

Additional copies of this book are available for purchase by calling toll-free 1-800-765-6955 or by visiting AdventistBookCenter.com.

Library of Congress Cataloging-in-Publication Data

Names: Reid, G. Edward, 1945- author.
Title: Managing for the master / G Edward Reid.
Description: Nampa, Idaho : Pacific Press Publishing Association, [2022] |
    Summary: "Managing for the Master is a review of the stewardship principles
    involved in a person's relationship with God. These principles, derived from
    Scripture, instruct the Christian on how to trust God and be financially faithful
    to Him"— Provided by publisher.
Identifiers: LCCN 2022019341 (print) | LCCN 2022019342 (ebook) |
    ISBN 9780816368655 (paperback) | ISBN 9780816368662 (ebook)
Subjects: LCSH: Christian giving. | Christian stewardship. |
    Finance, Personal—Religious aspects—Christianity.
Classification: LCC BV772 .R375 2022 (print) | LCC BV772 (ebook) | DDC
    248/.6—dc23/eng/20220622
LC record available at https://lccn.loc.gov/2022019341
LC ebook record available at https://lccn.loc.gov/2022019342

August 2022

Dedication

This book is dedicated to God's children around the world,
who sincerely seek to do His will in the management
of that which He has entrusted to them.

Contents

Introduction

Without a knowledge of our position and status in Christ as believers, the chaos of this present world would almost be overwhelming. It is difficult for us to comprehend—much less understand and grasp—the relationship that our God, the great and awesome Creator, wants to have with us. "Behold what manner of love the Father has bestowed on us, that we should be called children of God!" (1 John 3:1). No earthly kinship to a royal family could equal this relationship that God has offered to us. Ellen White notes that "God's appointments and grants in our behalf are without limit. The throne of grace is itself the highest attraction because [it is] occupied by One who permits us to call Him Father."[1]

In this book, we will discover and review God's ideal in our relationship with Him and clearly see how we can develop a trust so deep that we will remain faithful to Him, even when we cannot buy or sell (see Revelation 13:17). Our management for God forms such a relationship with Him that it has eternal consequences.

In the providence of God, He is the One who gives us guidance on how to earn money and utilize it wisely. In the more than two thousand verses of Scripture that deal with money, possessions, and our attitudes toward them, God gives practical instructions on how to live above the stresses of life, manage in such a way as to understand what it means to be financially faithful, and eventually hear the words of commendation from Jesus Himself: "Well done, good and faithful servant" (Matthew 25:21).

---

1. Ellen G. White, *Testimonies for the Church*, vol. 6 (Mountain View, CA: Pacific Press®, 1948), 363

1

Part of God's Family

Behold what manner of love the Father has bestowed
on us, that we should be called children of God!
   —1 John 3:1

Being part of a loving and caring family is indeed a pleasant experience. A home where father, mother, and children share mutual honor and respect for each other and where each family member accepts and performs individual responsibilities is a blessing to all. Unfortunately, such families are in the minority of households today. Because of selfishness and other devil-inspired attitudes, many families get along like stray cats. In some cases, parents are absent from the home circle because of abandonment, incarceration, addiction, or work responsibilities. It is in this setting that God offers each of us hope for something better—much better. "The home that is beautified by love, sympathy, and tenderness is a place that angels love to visit, and where God is glorified. The influence of a carefully guarded Christian home in the years of childhood and youth is the surest safeguard against the corruptions of the world. In the atmosphere of such a home the children will learn to love both their earthly parents and their heavenly Father."[1] "The children of God are those who are partakers of His nature. It is not earthly rank, nor birth, nor nationality, nor religious privilege, which proves that we are members of the family of God; it is love, a love that embraces all humanity."[2]

Being part of God's family

Because of His great love, God calls those who believe in Him and accept His gracious gift of a better life now and the promise of eternal life to be His children. We know that God exists and is deeply concerned about us for many reasons. I see God's hand in my life in many ways. The four ways that help me the most all begin with the letter *p*:

1. Prayers answered. God has answered literally hundreds of my prayers—from small things, such as finding something that I have misplaced, to restoring the health of a friend or loved one.

2. Prophecies fulfilled. We know that God loves us and is in control of the things on Earth; the rise and fall of nations by His outline of this world's history gives us hope and encouragement.

3. Providential leading of God. I see God's providential leading in where I went to academy and college, how I met my wife, and where I have been called to work for His cause.

4. Promises fulfilled. There are literally hundreds of God's promises to His children in the Bible. All of them can be claimed and enjoyed by us. Joshua, Moses' assistant who led the children of Israel across the Jordan River and into the Promised Land, gave these encouraging words just before he died: "Behold, this day I am going the way of all the earth. And you know in all your hearts and in all your souls that not one thing has failed of all the good things which the LORD your God spoke concerning you. All have come to pass for you; not one word of them has failed" (Joshua 23:14).

Early in the ministry of Jesus, He gave His longest recorded sermon (Matthew 5–7). In it, He emphasized the importance of prayer and began by giving three concerns: Do not pray for show or to be seen by others. Do not pray your personal prayers in public. And do not say the same things over and over again. But pray like this:

"In this manner, therefore, pray:

"Our Father in Heaven,
Hallowed be Your name" (Matthew 6:9).

Jesus was frequently in prayer. Several months later, when He had been separated from His disciples for a period of time, they returned to join Him, and they found Him praying. When He finished praying, they asked Him, "Lord, teach us to pray" (Luke 11:1). Jesus repeated the same prayer privately to His disciples that He had given to the great crowd on the mountainside. Jesus told them to call His Father "Our Father in heaven" (verse 2). This idea is so incredible that it can only be understood and accepted by faith. The Sovereign of the universe asks us to call Him Father!

How we become part of God's family

Becoming part of God's family is a matter of faith, guided by the Holy Spirit. Paul calls the process *adoption*. Jesus calls it being *born again*. Paul explains the process this way: "For as many as are led by the Spirit of God, they are the sons of God. For ye have not received the spirit of bondage again to fear; but ye have received the Spirit of adoption, whereby we cry, Abba, Father. The Spirit itself beareth witness with our spirit, that we are the children of God: And if children, then heirs; heirs of God, and joint-heirs with Christ; if so be that we suffer with him, that we may be also glorified together" (Romans 8:14–17, KJV).

The Gospel of John, which has inspired thousands of readers to accept Christ as their personal Savior, contains a story about Nicodemus and his secret nighttime interview with Jesus. Nicodemus was a talented and highly educated man who held a position of responsibility in the Jewish nation. Ellen White describes the significance of the encounter this way: "In the interview with Nicodemus, Jesus unfolded the plan of salvation, and His mission to the world. In none of His subsequent discourses did He explain so fully, step by step, the work necessary to be done in the hearts of all who would inherit the kingdom of heaven. At the very beginning of His ministry He opened the truth to a member of the Sanhedrin, to the mind that was most receptive, and to an appointed teacher of the people."[3]

Jesus told the esteemed rabbi plainly, "Verily, verily, I say unto thee, Except a man be born again, he cannot see the kingdom of God. . . . Verily, verily, I say unto thee, Except a man be born of water and of the Spirit, he cannot enter into the kingdom of God" (John 3:3–5,

KJV). In both of these verses, the kingdom of God is at stake, so it is imperative that we understand what it means to be "born of water and of the Spirit." We recognize that being born of water is our public baptism by immersion as a testimony that we have acknowledged our sinful condition and have accepted Jesus as our Savior by repentance and confession.

Being born of the Spirit is something that we ask of God. Jesus told His followers: "If ye then, being evil, know how to give good gifts unto your children: how much more shall your heavenly Father give the Holy Spirit to them that ask him?" (Luke 11:13, KJV). Jesus further explained to Nicodemus that the work of the Spirit in the born-again experience is much like the action of the wind. We cannot see the wind, but we can see its effects. Ellen White describes the visible effect of inviting the Holy Spirit into our lives.

> While the wind is itself invisible, it produces effects that are seen and felt. So the work of the Spirit upon the soul will reveal itself in every act of him who has felt its saving power. When the Spirit of God takes possession of the heart, it transforms the life. Sinful thoughts are put away, evil deeds are renounced; love, humility, and peace take the place of anger, envy, and strife. Joy takes the place of sadness, and the countenance reflects the light of heaven. No one sees the hand that lifts the burden, or beholds the light descend from the courts above. The blessing comes when by faith the soul surrenders itself to God. Then that power which no human eye can see creates a new being in the image of God.[4]

Responsibilities and privileges of God's children

When we are born again and adopted into the family of God, we are endowed with privileges and responsibilities that we accept and practice while the Master is away. The first and primary task is what we refer to as the *Great Commission*. In a private meeting with His disciples, Jesus assured them of success. "And this gospel of the kingdom will be preached in all the world as a witness to all the nations, and then the end will come" (Matthew 24:14). A little later, He laid out their job description plainly. "And Jesus came and spake unto them, saying, All power is given unto me in heaven and in earth. Go ye therefore, and teach all nations, baptizing them in the name of the Father, and of the Son, and of the Holy Ghost: Teaching them to observe all things whatsoever I have commanded you: and, lo, I am with you alway, even unto the end of the world. Amen" (Matthew 28:18–20, KJV).

Jesus gave us two detailed parables that illustrate the privileges and responsibilities of His children in the management of His affairs while we await His return. The first is recorded in Matthew 25:14–30. In this story—the parable of the talents—an owner of goods is planning to take a trip to a distant country. He calls his own servants (or employees) and gives each one a portion of his assets, according to their ability, to manage while he is away. Then, "after a long time the lord of those servants came and settled accounts with them" (verse 19). This is a time of accounting—an audit of their management of his goods. In this parable, the faithful servants are praised and given the reward of entering into "the joy of your lord," which represents eternal life. The unfaithful servant is called "wicked and lazy" (verse 26) and therefore receives the reward of the wicked, which is eternal death. For modern believers, a "long time" is the period of time between the first and second advents of Jesus.

The second and similar parable is not as well known but makes many important points. It is recorded in Luke 19:11–27. In this story, the word *talents* is replaced by a currency term: "pounds" or "minas." (A *mina* was roughly equivalent to one hundred days' wages.)

> Therefore He said: "A certain nobleman went into a far country to receive for himself a kingdom and to return. So he called ten of his servants, delivered to them ten minas, and said to them, 'Do business till I come.' "
>
> "And so it was that when he returned, having received the kingdom, he then commanded these servants, to whom he had given the money, to be called to him, that he might know how much every man had gained by trading" (Luke 19:12, 13, 15).

In Luke's account, as in the account in Matthew 25, only the master's servants were given large sums of money. At the end of the designated time, only the results of three servants are reported. The first two had worked diligently and made a good profit for the nobleman and were rewarded accordingly. The third recognized that the mina was not his (verse 20) but had done nothing to invest it for his master. He is called a "wicked servant" (verse 22). In the sight of Heaven, those who accomplish nothing with the talents entrusted to them are "wicked" and are certain to reap the reward of the wicked, which is the loss of eternal life. So, managing for the Master is a big deal—a really big deal.

Recognizing God's ownership

Ellen White notes that the initial step in partnering with God is recognizing His ownership. "That which lies at the foundation of business integrity and of true success is the recognition of God's ownership. The Creator of all things, He is the original proprietor. We are His stewards. All that we have is a trust from Him, to be used according to His direction."[5]

As Christians, we have the wonderful assurance that the God we serve rules in the heavens above and on the earth beneath. We serve the Creator and Sustainer. His power is described in Psalm 33:6, 9: "By the word of the LORD were the heavens made; and all the host of them by the breath of his mouth. . . . For he spake, and it was done; he commanded, and it stood fast" (KJV).

By the testimony of Scripture, we understand that it was Christ Himself who was the active agent in Creation. "In the beginning was the Word, and the Word was with God, and the Word was God. . . . All things were made by him; and without him was not any thing made that was made. . . . And the Word was made flesh, and dwelt among us, (and we beheld his glory, the glory as of the only begotten of the Father,) full of grace and truth" (John 1:1, 3, 14, KJV).

Creator equals Owner

In the two parables we have mentioned in this chapter—the parable of the minas (Luke 19) and the parable of the talents (Matthew 25)—it is explicitly clear that the servants who were given responsibilities knew that they were dealing with the assets of the master and not their own money. In addition, many Bible references underscore this fact. For example, Psalm 24:1 states, "The earth is the LORD's, and the fulness thereof; the world, and they that dwell therein" (KJV). And Psalm 50:12 adds, "If I were hungry, I would not tell thee: for the world is mine, and the fulness thereof" (KJV).

Many of Jesus' parables deal with money and material possessions or our attitudes toward them. There are well over two thousand biblical references that deal with this topic. In the New King James Version, there are fewer than five hundred on faith and less than four hundred mentions of prayer. Obviously, God thinks knowledge about money is important to His children and their management for Him in His kingdom business.

Jesus contrasts the competing power of money with God by stating, *"No one can serve two masters; for either he will hate the one and love the other, or else he will be loyal to the one and despise the other. You cannot serve God and mammon [money, wealth, riches]"* (Matthew 6:24; emphasis added). There are few places in Scripture where God makes such a direct comparison. Yet the competition is real. Money competes for our interest, time, and energy. It easily distracts us from more important priorities.

When addressing the talents that God gave to His own servants, Ellen White reported,

I was shown that the parable of the talents has not been fully understood. This important lesson was given to the disciples for the benefit of Christians living in the last days. And these talents do not represent merely the ability to preach and instruct from the word of God. The parable applies to the temporal means which God has entrusted to His people. Those to whom the five and the two talents were given, traded and doubled that which was committed to their trust. God requires those who have possessions here, to put their money out to usury for Him—to put it into the cause to spread the truth.[6]

Since inspired counsel makes it clear that we, as God's children, are partners with the Master, this book will share in practical detail the biblical principles of money and life management. God has shown how we can share in the joy of service for Him.

The Word of God informs us of the temptations and allurements of Satan. "But those who desire to be rich fall into temptation and a snare, and into many foolish and harmful lusts which drown men in destruction and perdition. For the love of money is a root of all kinds of evil, for which some have strayed from the faith in their greediness, and pierced themselves through with many sorrows" (1 Timothy 6:9, 10). Ellen White adds, "The love of money, the desire for wealth, is the golden chain that binds them [people] to Satan."[7]

> Christ gave His own life, that all the disloyal and disobedient might realize the truth of the promise given in the first chapter of John: "As many as received him, to them gave he power to become the sons of God, even to them that believe on his name" (John 1:12). Tell it over and over again. We may become the sons of God, members of the royal family, children of the heavenly King. All who accept Jesus Christ and hold the beginning of their confidence firm unto the end will be heirs of God and joint heirs with Christ to "an inheritance incorruptible, and undefiled, and that fadeth not away."[8]

"Those who decide to do nothing in any line that will displease God, will know, after presenting their case before Him, just what course to pursue. And they will receive not only wisdom, but strength. Power for obedience, for service, will be imparted to them, as Christ has promised."[9]

---

1. Ellen G. White, *The Adventist Home* (Nashville, TN: Southern Pub. Assn., 1952), 19.

2. Ellen G. White, *Thoughts From the Mount of Blessing* (Mountain View, CA: Pacific Press®, 1956), 75.

3. Ellen G. White, *The Desire of Ages* (Mountain View, CA: Pacific Press®, 1940), 176.

4. White, 173.

5. Ellen G. White, *Education* (Mountain View, CA: Pacific Press®, 1952), 137.

6. Ellen G. White, *Testimonies for the Church*, vol. 1 (Mountain View, CA: Pacific Press®, 1948), 197.

7. Ellen G. White, *Steps to Christ* (Nampa, ID: Pacific Press®, 1999), 44.

8. Ellen G. White, *That I May Know Him* (Washington, DC: Review and Herald®, 1964), 70.

9. White, *Desire of Ages*, 668.

2

God's Covenants With Us

"Now it shall come to pass, if you diligently obey the voice of the LORD your God, to observe carefully all His commandments which I command you today, that the LORD your God will set you high above all nations of the earth. And all these blessings shall come upon you and overtake you, because you obey the voice of the LORD your God."
—Deuteronomy 28:1, 2

Contracts between business enterprises keep the world of commerce running smoothly and efficiently. Contracts are so basic to the function of society that most law schools require a course in contracts for all first-year students, right along with real property, torts, and civil procedure. Even as individuals, we use contracts more than we realize. For example, if your car needs gas, you look for a gas station. You notice a sign that says $4.29. This means that the filling station has gas for sale at $4.29 per gallon. If you stop and fill up your car, you have accepted the offer and agree to pay the advertised price for the amount you purchase.

Some sales contracts follow a period of negotiation. If you need a car and see a used one parked along a road with a for sale sign on it, you might stop and ask the owner, "What is the price you are asking for the car?" If the owner says, "Five thousand dollars," you might say, "I will offer you forty-five hundred dollars." Frequently, after a short period of discussion, you agree on a price of $4,750. The owner wanted to receive more but was willing to sell for less, and you wanted to pay less but were willing to pay more. You both compromise and strike a bargain, and the contract is made.

We serve an awesome God who keeps His promises and His covenants with His children. "He has sent redemption to His people; He has commanded His covenant forever: holy and awesome is His name" (Psalm 111:9). God is straightforward in His dealings with us. He stoops to our level and comes to the place of making contracts with us—in writing! That is why it is important to carefully and prayerfully study God's Word to discover the promises and contracts He offers us.

Most of God's contracts are bilateral, which means that both parties—God and man—have a part to perform. A bilateral contract states that, "If you do this, I will do that," or the other way around: "I will do this if you do that." This is easily seen in Deuteronomy 28:1, 2, as cited at the beginning of this chapter.

A rarer type of contract is a unilateral contract, which states, "I will do this whether or not you do anything." This unilateral type of contract was demonstrated by the United States during the Cold War. Though other countries were also involved in the negotiations for nuclear disarmament, the US stated, in essence, "Whether other nuclear powers do anything about disarmament, we will cut our arsenal to so many." A few of God's contracts with all humankind are unilateral. For example, "He makes His sun rise on the evil and on the good, and sends rain on the just and on the unjust" (Matthew 5:45). Whether or not we do anything, we can count on God for sunshine and rain.

Following the Flood, God promised Noah and all humankind,

> "While the earth remains,
> Seedtime and harvest,
> Cold and heat,
> Winter and summer,
> And day and night
> Shall not cease" (Genesis 8:22).

As promised, the seasons continue to come and go. God also promised humankind and "every beast of the earth" (Genesis 9:11) that when we see a rainbow in the clouds, it is the sign of His covenant with us that there will never be another flood to cover all the earth (verses 9–16). No matter how wicked humankind becomes, there will never be another worldwide flood. This is God's unilateral contract with men and animals.

In this chapter, we will review some significant bilateral contracts between God and His children. These contracts concern only those who believe in God and are part of His family.

The salvation contract
The salvation contract that offers forgiveness of our sins and eternal life with God is basic to all of His contracts. This bilateral contract was explained to Nicodemus during his secret nighttime visit with Jesus. Note the contract elements in John 3:16: "For God so loved the world that He gave His only begotten Son, that whoever believes in Him should not perish but have everlasting life." God's part is that He loved the world, gave His only Son, and offers eternal life to whoever believes—our part—in Him.

Ellen White has noted, "The whole world is embraced in the contract of the great plan of redemption."[1] The words *whoever* and *the world* mean that Christ's substitutionary death on Calvary made salvation possible for every person that has ever lived or ever will live. Forgiveness and eternal life are available to everyone! Does that mean that everyone will be saved? No. The gift of salvation is offered and available to all humankind, but it must be accepted by faith to be realized. Some people believe in universalism, which is the belief that all humankind will be saved eventually. This belief would make the salvation contract a unilateral contract in which God would say, "I will save you—no matter what you believe or how you live." But this concept is not what the Bible teaches.

Jesus clearly taught that, though His substitutionary death was for all humankind, many people are traveling the broad way to destruction and eternal death, and only a few people are traveling the narrow way that leads to eternal life. "Enter by the narrow gate; for wide is the gate and broad is the way that leads to destruction, and there are many who go in by it. Because narrow is the gate and difficult is the way which leads to life, and there are few who find it" (Matthew 7:13, 14). Later, in the same chapter, Jesus points out that just calling ourselves Christians does not fulfill our part of the contract. "Not everyone who says to Me, 'Lord, Lord,' shall enter the kingdom of heaven, but he who does the will of My Father in heaven. Many will say to Me in that day, 'Lord, Lord, have we not prophesied in Your name, cast out demons in Your name, and done many wonders in Your name?' And then I will declare to them, 'I never knew you; depart from Me, you who practice lawlessness' " (verses 21–23).

Jesus concluded His sermon on the mount with a vivid illustration of our part in the salvation contract.

"Therefore whoever hears these sayings of Mine, and does them, I will liken him to a wise man who built his house on the rock: and the rain descended, the floods came, and the winds blew and beat on that house; and it did not fall, for it was founded on the rock.

"But everyone who hears these sayings of Mine, and does not do them, will be like a foolish man who built his house on the sand: and the rain descended, the floods came, and the winds blew and beat on that house; and it fell. And great was its fall" (verses 24–27).

A simple response of loving obedience to God's commandments makes the salvation contract complete.

Blessings or curses

Notwithstanding the trials and temptations of life, the choices we make and our responses to God's promises determine whether we live lives of blessings or curses. This is the theme of the book of Deuteronomy. It is the written account of Moses' farewell messages to the second generation of Israelites, following the forty years of wandering in the wilderness. These messages were given on the plains of Moab, just east of Jericho. The primary focus of Deuteronomy is the counsel to obey

God and receive His blessings. Moses portrays God as One who has the ability and the desire to care for His people.

Deuteronomy 28 is one large bilateral contract—the details of which are clearly spelled out. There are fourteen verses outlining amazing blessings and fifty-four verses recording the curses that follow disobedience. Notice the contract language in verses 1 and 13; it has been italicized.

"Now it shall come to pass, if you diligently obey the voice of the Lord *your God, to observe carefully all His commandments which I command you today, that the* Lord *your God will set you high above all nations of the earth.* And all these blessings shall come upon you and overtake you, because you obey the voice of the Lord your God:

"Blessed shall you be in the city, and blessed shall you be in the country.

"Blessed shall be the fruit of your body, the produce of your ground and the increase of your herds, the increase of your cattle and the offspring of your flocks.

"Blessed shall be your basket and your kneading bowl.

"Blessed shall you be when you come in, and blessed shall you be when you go out.

"The Lord will cause your enemies who rise against you to be defeated before your face; they shall come out against you one way and flee before you seven ways.

"The Lord will command the blessing on you in your storehouses and in all to which you set your hand, and He will bless you in the land which the Lord your God is giving you.

"The Lord will establish you as a holy people to Himself, just as He has sworn to you, if you keep the commandments of the Lord your God and walk in His ways. Then all peoples of the earth shall see that you are called by the name of the Lord, and they shall be afraid of you. And the Lord will grant you plenty of goods, in the fruit of your body, in the increase of your livestock, and in the produce of your ground, in the land of which the Lord swore to your fathers to give you. The Lord will open to you His good treasure, the heavens, to give the rain to your land in its season, and to bless all the work of your hand. You shall lend to many nations, but you shall not borrow. *And the LORD will make you the head and not the tail; you shall be above only, and not be beneath, if you heed the commandments of the LORD your God, which I command you today, and are careful to observe them.* So you shall not turn aside from any of the words which I command you this day, to the right or the left, to go after other gods to serve them" (Deuteronomy 28:1–14).

The bare bones of the blessing contract are simple: If we diligently obey and carefully observe God's commandments, He will give us abundant and miraculous blessings. God will care for our health, family, safety, livelihood, finances, property, and more.

The fifty-four verses of curses (verses 15–68) are the opposite of the blessings God gives; they also point out many blessings that we take for granted and rarely acknowledge. If perchance you have been living on the curse side of the contract, Ezekiel says there is hope for you. " 'Repent, and turn from all your transgressions, so that iniquity will not be your ruin. Cast away from you all the transgressions which you have committed, and get yourselves a new heart and a new spirit. For why should you die, O house of Israel? For I have no pleasure in the death of one who dies,' says the Lord GOD. 'Therefore turn and live!' " (Ezekiel 18:30–32).

The blessing of putting God first
The Bible is abundantly clear that God does not need our money. Then why does He ask us as His managers to put Him first? Apparently, God asks for the first portion of our increase so that He can bless the rest. If we leave our Creator and Father till last, there would not be much left to bless. One of my favorite contract promises is recorded in Proverbs 3:5–10. It is practical in its application, easy to understand, and simple to comply with on our part. Our part is faith and trust.

If you are concerned about what course to follow in the current state of conditions in the world, Proverbs 3 recommends,

> Trust in the LORD with all your heart,
> And lean not on your own understanding;
> In all your ways acknowledge Him,
> And He shall direct your paths (verses 5, 6).

Three verses later, Solomon records God's promise of provision for those who put Him in first place.

> Honor the LORD with your possessions,
> And with the firstfruits of all your increase;
> So your barns will be filled with plenty,
> And your vats will overflow with new wine (verses 9, 10).

This amazing contract-promise declares that if we put God first in our resource management, He will see to it that our storage facilities will be filled to the point of overflowing.

One of the most well-known bilateral contracts between God and His children is the tithe and offering contract that is recorded in Malachi 3:7–12. This contract is straightforward, explicit, and in writing, and the results are measurable. We will cover the tithe contract in some detail in the next chapter, but I mention it here because it is an integral part of our management contract with God.

God cares about our needs

God's attributes and care for His children are a source of wonder and amazement as we study His Word. His works of creation and redemption and His promise to come again to restore all things are wonderful. But His love also provides for our needs and sustains us on a daily basis. This aspect of God's goodness is mentioned many times in the Bible and is explained in some detail in the heart of the Sermon on the Mount in Matthew 6:19–34.

Jesus began His financial management counsel by saying, "Do not lay up for yourselves treasures on earth, where moth and rust destroy and where thieves break in and steal; but lay up for yourselves treasures in heaven, where neither moth nor rust destroys and where thieves do not break in and steal" (Matthew 6:19, 20). The counsel is plain.

Storing up treasures on Earth is not smart because it is not safe here. And we know that hoarded wealth will get burned up when Jesus returns. We are told, "But the day of the Lord will come as a thief in the night, in which the heavens will pass away with a great noise, and the elements will melt with fervent heat; both the earth and the works that are in it will be burned up" (2 Peter 3:10).

Jesus' positive counsel in Matthew 6:20 is to store up treasure in heaven. But how do we do that? There are at least two ways to store up treasure in heaven. Jesus told the rich young ruler, "Give to the poor, and you will have treasure in heaven" (Matthew 19:21). A second way is to support the cause of God financially. "Every opportunity to help a brother in need, or to aid the cause of God in the spread of the truth, is a pearl that you can send beforehand and deposit in the bank of heaven for safekeeping."[2]

Interestingly, in God's counsel to us, He has put our needs first— as one of the three proper uses of money. "Money has great value, because it can do great good. In the hands of God's children it is food for the hungry, drink for the thirsty, and clothing for the naked. It is a defense for the oppressed, and a means of help to the sick. But money is of no more value than sand, only as it is put to use in providing for the necessities of life, in blessing others, and advancing the cause of Christ."[3]

Since we all need food, clothing, and the other necessities of life, it seems only natural that we should be concerned about these things. But there is no need to worry because, just like the promise of Proverbs 3:9, 10, Matthew 6:31–33 assures us that if we seek God first, He will make sure that our needs are met: "Therefore do not worry, saying, 'What shall we eat?' or 'What shall we drink?' or 'What shall we wear?' For after all these things the Gentiles seek. For your heavenly Father knows that you need all these things. But seek first the kingdom of God and His righteousness, and all these things shall be added to you."

1. Ellen G. White, *Sermons and Talks*, vol. 2 (Silver Spring, MD: Ellen G. White Estate, 1994), 329.

2. Ellen G. White, *Testimonies for the Church*, vol. 3 (Mountain View, CA: Pacific Press®, 1948), 249.

3. Ellen G. White, *Christ's Object Lessons* (Washington, DC: Review and Herald®, 1941), 351.

The Tithing Contract

3

"Yet from the days of your fathers
You have gone away from My ordinances
And have not kept them.
Return to Me, and I will return to you,"
Says the LORD of hosts.
"But you said,
'In what way shall we return?'

"Will a man rob God?
Yet you have robbed Me!
But you say,
'In what way have we robbed You?'
In tithes and offerings.
You are cursed with a curse,
For you have robbed Me,
Even this whole nation.
Bring all the tithes into the storehouse,
That there may be food in My house,
And try Me now in this,"
Says the LORD of hosts,
"If I will not open for you the windows of heaven
And pour out for you such blessing
That there will not be room enough to receive it.

"And I will rebuke the devourer for your sakes,
So that he will not destroy the fruit of your ground,
Nor shall the vine fail to bear fruit for you in the field,"
Says the LORD of hosts.
        —Malachi 3:7–11

Malachi 3:7–11 contains the basic elements of the tithe contract. According to verses 7 and 8, the tithing experience is part of our relationship with God and is, therefore, a vital part of our spiritual life. Verses 7–9 state that if we are negligent in being faithful with our tithes and offerings, we have left God and are subject to the curses of Deuteronomy 28:15–68. It is likely that the prophet Malachi served Israel during the time between Nehemiah's two terms as governor. When Nehemiah returned to Judah, he found God's people in deep apostasy: they were lax in their Sabbath keeping, had intermarried with heathen people, and had failed to financially support the work of God with their tithes and offerings. The people had defaulted on their covenant (contract) with God, but God was still willing to keep His end of the contract.

The remedy for the breached contract continues in Malachi 3:10, 11. God says that if we bring as part of our worship experience all the tithes—the whole tithe and an honest tithe—to the storehouse, the place from which church workers are paid, there will be plenty in His house. Then God offers this challenge and an accompanying promise:

> "Try [test] Me now in this" . . .
> "[And see] if I will not open for you the windows of heaven
> And pour out for you such blessing
> That there will not be room enough to receive it.
>
> "And I will rebuke the devourer for your sakes" (verses 10, 11).

Ellen White notes, "In the third chapter of Malachi is found the contract God has made with man. Here the Lord specifies the part He will act in bestowing His great gifts on those who will make a faithful return to Him in tithes and offerings."[1]

The terms of the tithing contract are clear and succinct. If we return to God with repentance and obedience (our part), He will return to us with blessing (His part). If we are faithful with our tithes and offerings and prove Him in this (our part), He will open the windows of heaven and pour out for us more blessings than we need, so we will have a surplus that we can use to help others and advance the cause of God; His house will be supplied; *and* He will rebuke the devourer (Satan) for us (God's part).

Wow! What a deal! This looks like a lopsided contract in our favor. What individual or family could afford to go it on their own and lose out on all of these blessings?

The history of tithing

What exactly is *tithe*? *Tithe* is the tenth part of our income—or our increase, if we are self-employed. We understand that this is the part of our God-given increase that He claims as His own. We know that *tithe* means a tenth because the words for *tithe* and *tenth* are used interchangeably in both the Old and New Testaments.

The first mention of tithe in the Bible is in Genesis 14:20, when Abram gave Melchizedek, the priest of the Most High God, "a tithe of all" the spoils of Sodom, which he and his allies had retaken. It is interesting that the last mention of tithe in the Bible is in Hebrews 7:1–10. This is the New Testament recounting of the story of Abraham and his encounter with Melchizedek. In this account, we are told, "The patriarch Abraham gave a *tenth* of the spoils" (verse 4; emphasis added).

A further point that we learn from this story is that tithe was not just a Jewish ordinance associated with the Levitical priesthood. Melchizedek was God's priest who received tithe before the tribe of Levi existed. The final mention of tithe in Hebrews 7 states, "Our Lord arose from Judah, of which tribe Moses spoke nothing concerning priesthood. . . . [He is] a priest forever according to the order of Melchizedek" (verses 14, 17). Abraham's tithing experience occurred more than four thousand years ago and more than four hundred years before God gave His laws in written form through Moses.

The second mention of tithing also comes from the book of Genesis. This story is recorded in chapter 28 and involves the flight of Jacob, who was fleeing for his life after tricking his brother, Esau, out of his birthright. After two days of running, Jacob stopped to rest for the night. He was exhausted, lonely, and frightened. But his greatest concern was his relationship with God. Before going to sleep, he confessed his sin, asked for protection, and prayed for some evidence that he was not forsaken by God.[2] The Bible records the rest of this amazing experience.

Then he dreamed, and behold, a ladder was set up on the earth, and its top reached to heaven; and there the angels of God were ascending and descending on it.

And behold, the LORD stood above it and said: "I am the LORD God of Abraham your father and the God of Isaac; the land on which you lie I will give to you and your descendants. Also your descendants shall be as the dust of the earth; you shall spread abroad to the west and the east, to the north and the south; and in you and in your seed all the families of the earth shall be blessed. Behold, I am with you and will keep you wherever you go, and will bring you back to this land; for I will not leave you until I have done what I have spoken to you."

Then Jacob awoke from his sleep and said, "Surely the LORD is in this place, and I did not know it." And he was afraid and said, "How awesome is this place! This is none other than the house of God, and this is the gate of heaven!"

Then Jacob rose early in the morning, and took the stone that he had put at his head, set it up as a pillar, and poured oil on top of it. And he called the name of that place Bethel; but the name of that city had been Luz previously. Then Jacob made a vow, saying, "If God will be with me, and keep me in this way that I am going, and give me bread to eat and clothing to put on, so that I come back to my father's house in peace, then the LORD shall be my God. And this stone which I have set as a pillar shall be God's house, and of all that You give me I will surely give a tenth to You" (Genesis 28:12–22).

Jacob's vow to be a faithful tither was not an attempt to buy God's favor. He was simply responding to the promises God had already made to him. As an example to believers in all ages, this young man begins his journey through life by taking God as his partner.

As we have noted above, God's children had been keeping His commandments for centuries before they were formally delivered at Mount Sinai. The tithe command is recorded as follows: "And all the tithe of the land, whether of the seed of the land or of the fruit of the tree, is the LORD's. It is holy to the LORD. . . . And concerning the tithe of the herd or the flock, of whatever passes under the rod, the tenth one shall be holy to the Lord" (Leviticus 27:30, 32). In this passage, *tithe* and *tenth* are given in the same setting.

The use of the tithe

We understand that the tithe is holy and belongs to God. This means that He can do whatever He wants to with it. But He has clearly told us what He wants *us* to do with His tithe. "Behold, I have given the children of Levi all the tithes in Israel as an inheritance in return for the work which they perform, the work of the tabernacle of meeting" (Numbers 18:21). From the beginning, God pays religious workers with His tithe. We are told,

> The portion that God has reserved for Himself is not to be diverted to any other purpose than that which He has specified. Let none feel at liberty to retain their tithe, to use according to their own judgment. They are not to use it for themselves in an emergency, nor to apply it as they see fit, even in what they may regard as the Lord's work. . . .
>
> The tithe is sacred, reserved by God for Himself. It is to be brought into His treasury to be used to sustain the gospel laborers in their work.[3]

According to this counsel, we should not use our tithe to pave the parking lot at church, buy choir robes, pay for children's tuition, or build a new church. Our tithes should be clearly marked as tithe and used to support gospel workers. Accordingly, in harmony with this Bible principle, the Seventh-day Adventist Church has designated the local conference as the storehouse to which tithes should be returned and from which gospel ministry workers receive their salaries. In addition, the local conference gives support to the furtherance of the gospel in all the world. For the convenience of church members, as part of their worship experience, tithes are returned through the local church where membership is held, and the local treasurer forwards all tithes to the conference storehouse from which religious workers are paid. This system, outlined by God, has enabled His church to have a global and ever-growing impact on the world.

An honest tithe

Our tithe is not an offering that is discretionary. Our offerings can be small or large and given whenever and to whatever we choose to support to show our thanks to God for His blessings. Tithe, on the other hand, is holy and belongs to God. Ellen White makes the point: " 'Bring ye all the tithes into the storehouse' (Malachi 3:10), is God's command. No appeal is made to gratitude or to generosity. This is a matter of simple honesty. The tithe is the Lord's; and He bids us return to Him that which is His own."[4]

An honest or faithful tithe incorporates the biblical principles we have covered in this chapter:

1. Tithe is a tenth (10 percent) of our income or increase (Leviticus 27:30, 32; Genesis 28:22; Hebrews 7:2). We are not to give just a token amount but "all the tithes" (Malachi 3:10) or the whole tithe.

2. Tithe is to be taken from the first part of our expense account (Proverbs 3:9; Matthew 6:33). "Not only does the Lord claim the tithe as His own, but He tells us *how* it should be reserved for Him. He says, 'Honor the Lord with thy substance, and with the *first fruits* of all thine increase.' This does not teach that we are to spend our means on ourselves, and bring to the Lord the remnant, even though it should be otherwise an honest tithe. Let God's portion be first set apart."[5]

3. Tithe is brought as a part of our worship experience (Malachi 3:10). David promised,

> I will pay my vows to the LORD
> Now in the presence of all His people,
> In the courts of the LORD's house,
> In the midst of you, O Jerusalem (Psalm 116:18, 19).

This was the practice of all the faithful in Israel.

4. Tithe is returned to the "storehouse"—the place from which church workers are paid (Malachi 3:10).

The central storehouse

We see that tithe is a tenth of our income or increase and belongs to God. So what should we do with it? Here again, the Bible is clear and specific. We are told that we should "*bring all the tithes* [the whole tithe] *into the storehouse*, that there may be food in My house" (Malachi 3:10; emphasis added). This begs the question, What and where is the storehouse? By studying the Bible, we see that God's people in Old Testament times had no problem identifying the storehouse. They all went there three times a year!

Just before he died, Moses gathered all Israel together and gave them a series of sermons or public presentations. They are recorded for us in the Bible as the book of Deuteronomy. He stated that even though the children of Israel were to be settled and scattered all over Canaan, they were to assemble three times a year at the Lord's house for praise, worship, and the delivery of their tithes and offerings. "But when ye go over Jordan, and dwell in the land which the LORD your God giveth you to inherit, and when he giveth you rest from all your enemies round about, so that ye dwell in safety; then there shall be a place which the LORD your God shall choose to cause his name to dwell there; thither shall ye bring all that I command you; your burnt offerings, and your sacrifices, your tithes, and the heave offering of your hand, and all your choice vows which ye vow unto the LORD" (Deuteronomy 12:10, 11, KJV).

Three times each year all the males in Israel were to appear before the Lord: Passover, the Feast of Weeks, and the Feast of Tabernacles. "Three times in a year shall all thy males appear before the LORD thy God in the place which he shall choose; in the feast of unleavened bread, and in the feast of weeks, and in the feast of tabernacles: and they shall not appear before the LORD empty: every man shall give as he is able, according to the blessing of the LORD thy God which he hath given thee" (Deuteronomy 16:16, 17, KJV; see also Exodus 23:14–17).

Anciently the Lord instructed His people to assemble three times a year for His worship. To these holy convocations the children of Israel came, bringing to the house of God their tithes, their sin offerings, and their offerings of gratitude. They met to recount God's mercies, to make known His wonderful works, and to offer praise and thanksgiving to His name. And they were to unite in the sacrificial service which pointed to Christ as the Lamb of

God that taketh away the sin of the world. Thus they were to be preserved from the corrupting power of worldliness and idolatry. Faith and love and gratitude were to be kept alive in their hearts, and through their association together in this sacred service they were to be bound closer to God and to one another.[6]

After the tithes were brought to the central storehouse, the Levites distributed the tithes to their brethren all over the land of Israel (2 Chronicles 31:11–21; Nehemiah 12:44–47; 13:4–13).

Here is the bottom line: The Israelites gave at least one-fourth of their income to God in the form of tithes, thank offerings, support of the temple, and gifts to the poor.[7] In addition, most of these donations were personally delivered by each family, in-kind or cash equivalents, to the central storehouse, which was first in Shiloh and then in Jerusalem. This personal delivery system required the Israelites to be away from home and work for at least one month each year. Yet giving 25 percent and being away from home for one month were actually the basis for their prosperity and blessing—and they knew it!

A test of loyalty
Ellen White draws a parallel between the test of the tree of knowledge of good and evil for Adam and Eve and the practice of tithing for the Christian.

> The Lord placed our first parents in the Garden of Eden. He surrounded them with everything that could minister to their happiness, and He bade them acknowledge Him as the possessor of all things. In the garden He caused to grow every tree that was pleasant to the eye or good for food; but among them He made one reserve. Of all else, Adam and Eve might freely eat; but of this one tree God said, "Thou shalt not eat of it." Here was the test of their gratitude and loyalty to God.
>
> So [or in like manner] the Lord has imparted to us heaven's richest treasure in giving us Jesus. With Him He has given us all things richly to enjoy. The productions of the earth, the bountiful harvests, the treasures of gold and silver, are His gifts. Houses and

lands, food and clothing, He has placed in the possession of men. He asks us to acknowledge Him as the Giver of all things; and for this reason He says, Of all your possessions I reserve a tenth for Myself, besides gifts and offerings, which are to be brought into My storehouse.[8]

So why did Adam and Eve eat from the forbidden tree? And why are some Christians unfaithful in returning God's holy tithe? Could there be a parallel here as well? Here is the reason from Eden: "There was nothing poisonous in the fruit itself, and the sin was not merely in yielding to appetite. It was [1] distrust of God's goodness, [2] disbelief of His word, and [3] rejection of His authority, that made our first parents transgressors, and that brought into the world a knowledge of evil. It was this that opened the door to every species of falsehood and error."[9]

Today, human nature is much the same as it was in millennia past. We are prone to distrust God's goodness, disbelieve His Word, and reject His authority. Recognizing our fallen condition, God gently invites us to "taste and see that the LORD is good; blessed is the man who trusts in Him!" (Psalm 34:8).

---

1. Ellen G. White, " 'Bring an Offering Unto the Lord,' " *Review and Herald*, December 17, 1901, 1.

2. See Ellen G. White, *Patriarchs and Prophets* (Mountain View, CA: Pacific Press®, 1958), 183.

3. Ellen G. White, *Testimonies for the Church*, vol. 9 (Mountain View, CA: Pacific Press®, 1948), 247, 249.

4. Ellen G. White, *Education* (Oakland, CA: Pacific Press®, 1903), 138.

5. Ellen G. White, *Counsels on Stewardship* (Washington, DC: Review and Herald®, 1940), 81; emphasis in the original.

6. Ellen G. White, *Testimonies for the Church*, vol. 6 (Mountain View, CA: Pacific Press®, 1948), 39.

7. White, *Patriarchs and Prophets*, 527.

8. White, *Counsels on Stewardship*, 65.

9. White, *Education*, 25.

4

Offerings for Jesus

"They shall not appear before the LORD empty-handed. Every man shall give as he is able, according to the blessing of the LORD your God which He has given you."
—Deuteronomy 16:16, 17

Have you ever wondered why so many offerings are collected at church and what they all go for? Who hasn't? The simple explanation is that God uses all the offerings to accomplish ministry through the church.

Seventh-day Adventists understand that biblical stewardship designates tithes as holy funds to be used for the support of the gospel ministry and are distinct from other church offerings. In contrast to tithes, offerings are used at all levels of church ministry. Their first and primary use is for the operation and maintenance of the local church. Unlike tithes, offerings are a discretionary gift on the part of the giver—that is, one can choose to support any area of God's work with what he or she is impressed to give.

The Gospel of Matthew concludes with Jesus' great commission: "All authority has been given to Me in heaven and on earth. Go therefore and make disciples of all the nations, baptizing them in the name of the Father and of the Son and of the Holy Spirit, teaching them to observe all things that I have commanded you; and lo, I am with you always, even to the end of the age" (Matthew 28:18–20). This text is another example of God's contract with His followers: You take the gospel to the world, and I will always be with you. "God has done His part of the work for the salvation of men, and now He calls for the co-operation of the church. There are the blood of Christ, the word of truth, the Holy Spirit, on one hand, and there are the perishing souls on the other. Every follower of Christ has a part to act to bring men to accept the blessings heaven has provided. Let us closely examine ourselves and see if we have done this work."[1] Managing for God has great blessings but also has important responsibilities.

As Bible-believing Christians, we do not give because we have too much. We give in response to experienced grace and in thanksgiving for God's blessings. We give to the programs and areas we believe will advance the cause of God. We understand that since God is the rightful Owner of everything, once our needs are met with the resources that He has entrusted to us, we return the surplus to Him by helping others or making contributions to advance His cause.

It is satisfying to know that our church has a worldwide impact and that thousands are becoming members every week. Our financial faithfulness brings us God's wisdom and blessings and spreads the gospel to every corner of the earth.

Our worship experience includes bringing offerings to the Lord.

> Give to the LORD the glory due His name;
> Bring an offering, and come into His courts.
> Oh, worship the LORD in the beauty of holiness!
> Tremble before Him, all the earth (Psalm 96:8, 9).

The gift of Christ reveals the Father's heart. It testifies that, having undertaken our redemption, He will spare nothing, however dear, which is necessary to the completion of His work. . . .

. . . God planned the system of beneficence, in order that man might become like his Creator, benevolent and unselfish in character, and finally be a partaker with Christ of the eternal, glorious reward.[2]

"The Lord does not need our offerings. We cannot enrich Him by our gifts. Says the psalmist, 'All things come of Thee, and of Thine own have we given Thee.' Yet God permits us to show our appreciation of His mercies by self-sacrificing efforts to extend the same to others. This is the only way in which it is possible for us to manifest our gratitude and love to God. He has provided no other."[3]

Our offerings come from the 90 percent that remains in our possession after our tithe is returned to God. The Bible recorded several different types of offerings given by God's people. There were

- sin offerings given as a response to experienced grace;
- thank offerings given to recognize God's protection and His blessings of health, prosperity, and sustaining power;
- offerings for the poor; and
- offerings to build and maintain the house of worship.

With the possible exception of the temple tax, offerings were not given according to a percentage, as was the tithe. In many cases, such as the call to build the tabernacle, the heartfelt offerings would exceed the tithe. God's simple command was, "Every man shall give as he is able, according to the blessing of the LORD your God which He has given you" (Deuteronomy 16:17).

God considered the failure to bring offerings to the storehouse, in addition to tithe, as theft from Him. Obviously, that is where the sin offerings and temple support offerings would go. But unlike tithe, some of our offerings can be discretionary. In other words, we can designate a portion of our offerings to help the poor, orphans, and widows and projects we believe support the work of God on Earth.

We must remember that God is the Owner-Partner. We are managing partners. Everything belongs to God, and we manage His investments in partnership with Him. We acknowledge that relationship through our tithes, and we invest directly in His kingdom. We manage His assets as we invest them in His kingdom through our offerings and in the way we care for our families and those in need.

Jesus takes note of our offerings

Imagine you are a financial adviser. You have an appointment today with an elderly woman, whose husband died some time ago. She begins the interview by telling you this: "I am down to my last two dollars. I have no more money, the cupboards are bare, and these two dollars are all I have to live on. Yet I feel like I should put the whole two dollars in the church offering. What do you think?"

What do you think? What would you tell her? Maybe you would say something like this: "That is very generous of you, but remember that God does not need the money. He just wants our hearts. Remember that God gave you common sense and wants you to take care of yourself. He knows you have to eat. And He knows your heart—that you *want* to give. I am sure God would have you keep those two dollars and buy some food for tomorrow. He wants your needs to be met, and you cannot expect Him to send food from heaven if you give up the little money that He has provided, can you? After all, God wants us to do the sensible and responsible thing."

Doesn't this advice to this poor widow seem reasonable enough? Would you say anything differently? What would God say? In this case, we do not need to speculate—the Bible tells us exactly what He says.

In Mark 12:41–44, we find the story of the poor widow. "Now Jesus sat opposite the treasury and saw how the people put money into the treasury. And many who were rich put in much. Then one poor widow came and threw in two mites, which make a quadrans. So He called His disciples to Himself and said to them, 'Assuredly, I say to you that this poor widow has put in more than all those who have given to the treasury; for they all put in out of their abundance, but she out of her poverty put in all that she had, her whole livelihood.' "

The widow dropped two tiny copper coins, worth a fraction of a penny, into the temple offering box. This was the only money that she had. Jesus called His disciples together to teach them a lesson from the woman's actions. Did He question the wisdom of her actions? Did He say she should have been more sensible than to surrender her only remaining resources? No, He gave her an unqualified commendation: "Truly I tell you, this poor widow has put more into the treasury than all the others. They all gave of their wealth; but she, out of her poverty, put in everything—all she had to live on" (verse 44, NIV).

Jesus regarded the woman as wise. He set her up as a model for His disciples to follow. He actually enshrined her example in the Word of God so believers in future generations might emulate her faith, commitment, and sacrificial generosity.

In his account of this story, Mark observes that "Jesus sat down opposite the place where the offerings were put and watched the crowd putting their money into the temple treasury" (verse 41, NIV). Notice we are not told that "Jesus happened to see . . ." No, it seems that He deliberately watched to observe what the people were giving. Can you imagine the scene? How close do you think Jesus was to the offering box? Close enough to see some people put in large amounts.

Jesus was close enough to see two tiny copper coins (verse 42). He was interested enough in what was being given to make an immediate object lesson for His disciples about the true nature of trusting God as demonstrated in sacrificial financial giving (verses 43, 44).

This passage from Mark makes those of us who suppose that what we do with our money is our business and only our business feel terribly uncomfortable. What we do with our money is clearly God's business—He makes it His business. He does not apologize for watching with intense interest what we do with the money He has entrusted to us.[4]

How could I call myself a Christian, a disciple of Jesus, without ever coming to grips with the issue of money and possessions? Even a cursory reading of the New Testament shows this issue is at the heart of discipleship.

Ellen White makes an important point about the widow's mites. "She believed the service of the temple to be of God's appointment, and she was anxious to do her utmost to sustain it. She did what she could, and her act was to be a monument to her memory through all time, and her joy in eternity. Her heart went with her gift; its value was estimated, not by the worth of the coin, but by the love to God and the interest in His work that had prompted the deed."[5]

It is significant to note that the only offering Jesus ever commended was when this widow gave everything she had to a church that was soon to kill Him. In the following statement, Ellen White writes that givers will be blessed in spite of possible misuses by the church.

> I was shown that the recording angel makes a faithful record of every offering dedicated to God and put into the treasury, and also of the final result of the means thus bestowed. The eye of God takes cognizance of every farthing devoted to His cause, and of the willingness or reluctance of the giver. The motive in giving is also chronicled. Those self-sacrificing, consecrated ones who render back to God the things that are His, as He requires of them, will be rewarded according to their works. Even though the means thus consecrated be misapplied, so that it does not accomplish the object which the donor had in view—the glory of God and the salvation of souls—those who made the sacrifice in sincerity of soul, with an eye single to the glory of God, will not lose their reward.[6]

Cornelius

An angel from heaven was sent to visit a Roman centurion named Cornelius. The amazing story is found in Acts 10:1–6.

> There was a certain man in Caesarea called Cornelius, a centurion of what was called the Italian Regiment, a devout man and one who feared God with all his household, who gave alms generously to the people, and prayed to God always. About the ninth hour of the day he saw clearly in a vision an angel of God coming in and saying to him, "Cornelius!"
> And when he observed him, he was afraid, and said, "What is it, lord?"

So he said to him, "Your prayers and your alms have come up for a memorial before God. Now send men to Joppa, and send for Simon whose surname is Peter. He is lodging with Simon, a tanner, whose house is by the sea. He will tell you what you must do."

Joppa is about thirty-five miles south of Caesarea, which is two days' journey on foot. Keep this in mind as the story unfolds. There are some very remarkable facts in this story. Peter was in Joppa because he had been called there upon the death of Dorcas, whom, by the power of God, he raised from the dead. The same angel who visited Cornelius then went to Joppa and visited Peter.[7] Both men obeyed the instructions of the angel with marvelous results. It all started with prayerful and generous Cornelius.

Cornelius was not yet a follower of the Messiah, but he was a very generous person and was devoted to God and spent considerable time in prayer. The angel told him that the reason he had come from heaven was that his prayers and his alms had come up as a memorial before God. Ellen White notes:

> It is a wonderful favor for any man in this life to be commended of God as was Cornelius. And what was the ground of this approval?—"Thy prayers and thine alms are come up for a memorial before God" (Acts 10:4). . . .
>
> Prayer and almsgiving are closely linked together—the expression of love to God and to our fellow men. They are the outworking of the two great principles of the divine law, "Thou shalt love the Lord thy God with all thy heart, and with all thy soul, and with all thy mind, and with all thy strength"; and, "Thou shalt love thy neighbour as thyself" (Mark 12:30, 31). Thus while our gifts cannot recommend us to God or earn His favor, they are an evidence that we have received the grace of Christ. They are a test of the sincerity of our profession of love.[8]

God desires people to pray and to plan for the advancement of his work. But, like Cornelius, we are to unite praying with giving.

Our prayers and our alms are to come up before God as a memorial. Faith without works is dead; and without a living faith it is impossible to please God. While we pray, we are to give all we possibly can, both of our labor and our means, for the fulfilment of our prayers. If we act out our faith, we shall not be forgotten by God. He marks every deed of love and self-denial. He will open ways whereby we may show our faith by our works.[9]

Zacchaeus

It is important to look at how closely Jesus linked money with salvation. The first ten verses of Luke 19 tell the story of Zacchaeus. When Zacchaeus said he would give half of his money to the poor and pay back four times over to those he had cheated, Jesus did not merely say, "Good idea." He said, "Today salvation has come to this house" (verse 9). This is amazing! Jesus judged the reality of this man's salvation based on his willingness—no, his cheerful eagerness—to part with his money for the glory of God and the good of others. One encounter with Jesus transformed Zacchaeus from a selfish tax collector to a child of God!

The light of the gospel shining from the cross of Christ rebukes selfishness, and encourages liberality and benevolence. It should not be a lamented fact that there are increasing calls to give. God in His providence is calling His people out from their limited sphere of action, to enter upon greater enterprises. Unlimited effort is demanded at this time when moral darkness is covering the world. Many of God's people are in danger of being ensnared by worldliness and covetousness. They should understand that it is His mercy that multiplies the demands for their means. Objects that call benevolence into action must be placed before them, or they cannot pattern after the character of the great Exemplar.[10]

The future of giving

As we look to the future, giving will become more important than ever. "Those who really feel a deep interest in the advancement of the cause will not hesitate to invest money in the enterprise whenever and wherever it is needed."[11]

"In the last extremity, before this work shall close, thousands will be cheerfully laid upon the altar. Men and women will feel it a blessed privilege to share in the work of preparing souls to stand in the great day of God, and they will give hundreds as readily as dollars are given now."[12]

"Lay all upon His altar—self, property, and all, a living sacrifice. It will take all to enter glory. Lay up for yourselves treasure in heaven, where no thief can approach or rust corrupt. Ye must be partakers of Christ's sufferings here if ye would be partakers with Him of His glory hereafter."[13]

1. Ellen G. White, *Testimonies for the Church*, vol. 5 (Mountain View, CA: Pacific Press®, 1948), 610.

2. Ellen G. White, *Counsels on Stewardship* (Washington, DC: Review and Herald®, 1940), 14, 15.

3. White, 18.

4. Randy Alcorn, *Money, Possessions, and Eternity*, rev. ed. (Wheaton, IL: Tyndale House, 2003), 4–9.

5. Ellen G. White, *The Desire of Ages* (Mountain View, CA: Pacific Press®, 1940), 615.

6. Ellen G. White, *Testimonies for the Church*, vol. 2 (Mountain View, CA: Pacific Press®, 1948), 518.

7. Ellen G. White, *The Acts of the Apostles* (Mountain View, CA: Pacific Press®, 1911), 135.

8. Ellen G. White, *God's Amazing Grace* (Washington, DC: Review and Herald®, 1973), 86.

9. Ellen G. White, "An Appeal in Behalf of the Australasian Field," *Atlantic Union Gleaner*, June 17, 1903, 286 (2).

10. White, *Counsels on Stewardship*, 14.

11. Ellen G. White, *Testimonies for the Church*, vol. 4 (Mountain View, CA: Pacific Press®, 1948), 18.

12. White, *Counsels on Stewardship*, 40.

13. Ellen G. White, *The Faith I Live By* (Washington, DC: Review and Herald®, 1958), 359.

5

Dealing With Debt

*The rich rules over the poor, and the borrower
is servant [slave] to the lender.*
—Proverbs 22:7

The wicked borrows and does not repay.
—Psalm 37:21

Given all the stresses of life at this time in the great controversy, the devil complicates living even more by encouraging individuals and families to spend more than they earn and run into debt. Studies show that around 40 percent of couples who divorce point to financial difficulties as one of the major factors in the dissolution of their marriage.

Although debt seems to be a way of life in the West today, it should never be the norm for Christians. The Bible says *no* to debt. In the Scriptures, there are more than twenty-six references to being in debt, and all are negative. The Bible does not say it is a sin to borrow money, but it does talk about the consequences of doing so. Here are seven biblical principles about indebtedness:

1. Debt is a form of bondage. "The borrower is servant to the lender" (Proverbs 22:7). In the time of the patriarchs, more often than not, an individual became a slave precisely because he or she was a debtor. Not much has changed in four thousand years. Admittedly, we are no longer thrown into physical bondage, but too often, we have become slaves to material possessions through the overextension of credit.[1] "Many, very many, have not so educated themselves that they can keep their expenditures within the limit of their income. They do not learn to adapt themselves to circumstances, and they borrow and borrow again and again, and become overwhelmed in debt, and consequently they become discouraged and disheartened."[2] The best advice to avoid the bondage of borrowing is to follow these three rules:

A. Borrow only on items that *appreciate in value.*
B. Borrow with a *short-term loan.*
C. Borrow at the *best interest rate available.*[3]

2. Debt is a lack of contentment. "I have learned in whatever state I am, to be content" (Philippians 4:11). Paul also told the young Timothy, "Now godliness with contentment is great gain. For we brought nothing into this world, and it is certain we can carry nothing out. And having food and clothing, with these we shall be content" (1 Timothy 6:6–8). A lack of financial contentment is often reflected in our modern society in the attitudes we have toward debt. "Keeping up with the Joneses"—desiring what others have (covetousness) or wanting more than we already have (greediness)—frequently causes people to go into debt.[4]

3. Debt presumes on the future. "Now listen, you who say, 'Today or tomorrow we will go to this or that city, spend a year there, carry on business and make money.' Why, you do not even know what will happen tomorrow" (James 4:13, 14, NIV). This is a good working definition for *debt*: living today on the money you expect to earn in the future. Until World War II, few Americans carried loans over an extended period. In the 1930s, Congress enacted a law allowing the general public to procure home mortgages of twenty-five years. Previously, the longest home loans were around ten years, and car loans were no longer than one year. In America, we can now get home loans for up to fifty years. Only the Japanese "outloan" us with 100-year mortgages. Yet, in all of this, many do not know whether they can make their next payment.

4. Avoid get-rich-quick schemes. "A faithful man will abound with blessings, but he who hastens to be rich will not go unpunished" (Proverbs 28:20). "But those who desire to be rich fall into temptation and a snare, and into many foolish and harmful lusts which drown men in destruction and perdition. For the love of money is a root of all kinds of evil, for which some have strayed from the faith in their greediness, and pierced themselves through with many sorrows" (1 Timothy 6:9, 10). Get-rich-quick schemes flourish when two elements are present: One element is people who wish to profit financially from the ignorance, naïveté, or greed of others. The other is the desire on the part of a person to strike it rich with little effort and big dreams. When these meet, there is a big flash in the pan that quickly dies. Friendships end, and many people are hurt emotionally and financially. An additional tragedy with these devious plans is that, in most cases, the individuals have to borrow money to become involved. And when the scheme fails, they not only lose the borrowed money but often have to pay it back at high interest, thus putting their family under financial strain.[5]

5. Refuse to be surety for others (cosigning). The Bible is clear that we should not become responsible for the debt obligations of others. Solomon, the inspired wise man, warned against surety many times. Here are four of them.

A. "My son, if you become surety for your friend, if you have shaken hands in pledge for a stranger, you are snared by the words of your own mouth; you are taken by the words of your mouth. So do this, my son, and deliver yourself; for you have come into the hand of your friend: go and humble yourself; plead with your friend. Give no sleep to your eyes, nor slumber to your eyelids. Deliver yourself like a gazelle from the hand of the hunter, and like a bird from the hand of the fowler" (Proverbs 6:1–5).

B. "He who is surety for a stranger will suffer, but one who hates being surety is secure" (Proverbs 11:15).

C. "A man devoid of understanding shakes hands in a pledge, and becomes surety for his friend" (Proverbs 17:18).

D. "Do not be one of those who shakes hands in a pledge, one of those who is surety for debts" (Proverbs 22:26).

Surety usually occurs when a person with poor credit seeks a loan from a lending institution but does not qualify for the loan. The loan officer will tell the unqualified person that if he or she gets a friend with good credit to cosign the loan, the institution will grant the loan and hold the cosigner responsible in the event of default. Sometimes a fellow church member will come and ask you to cosign for him or her. Your response should be, "The Bible says I should never do that." Please understand that the Bible encourages us to be helpful to those in need, but we should not become responsible for their debts.

Parents are often asked by teenagers to cosign for the purchase of their first car. Adult children may ask their parents to cosign for a business loan. The same answer applies. It is appropriate to help others if you see a real need, but do not become surety for the debts of others. The Bible says this is a mistake. According to the Federal Trade Commission, 75 percent of those who cosigned for finance company loans ended up making the payments themselves.[6] Remember, if you cosign for someone, that debt is on your credit report until the loan is paid in full.

6. *Debt can erode our Christian witness.* "The wicked borrow and do not repay" (Psalm 37:21, NIV). It is impossible to tell your landlord that Jesus loves him and is the answer to all of his problems when he wonders why your Jesus has not convicted you to pay your last two months' rent.[7] A century ago Ellen White put it this way: "You bring a reproach upon the cause by locating in a place, where you indulge indolence for a time and then are obliged to run in debt for provision for your family. These your honest debts you are not always particular to pay, but, instead, move to another place. This is defrauding your neighbor. The world has a right to expect strict integrity in those who profess to be Bible Christians."[8]

7. *Debt imperils one's giving.* "Every man shall give as he is able, according to the blessing of the LORD your God which He has given you" (Deuteronomy 16:17). As you look at annual statistics about charitable contributions in our society, what should always surprise and

shock you is that the giving patterns of Christians and non-Christians are approximately the same amount—about 2.5 percent. Perhaps the biggest reason that the average American Christian does not return the 10 percent tithe and the offerings that God asks us to give Him is that they are in over their heads in debt.[9] In addition, many have never learned the biblical principles of tithing.

Is bankruptcy an alternative for the Christian?
People frequently ask, "If you are in over your head, isn't bankruptcy provided for in the Bible?" The answer is no! The verse frequently referred to is Deuteronomy 15:1, 2: "At the end of every seven years you shall grant a release of debts. And this is the form of the release: Every creditor who has lent anything to his neighbor shall release it; he shall not require it of his neighbor or his brother, because it is called the LORD's release." This counsel was given to creditors, not debtors. It was simply God's way of limiting long-term indebtedness to a maximum of seven years! And as we have already noted, "The wicked borrows and does not repay, but the righteous shows mercy and gives" (Psalm 37:21).

Bankruptcy laws were put in place to help those who faced catastrophic or overwhelming circumstances. But many today have abused the bankruptcy system because of their poor management. For the sake of your Christian witness and credit integrity, I rarely recommend bankruptcy and encourage a reorganization method at that point.

Families in over their heads with credit card debt often are bombarded by offers to lower their monthly payments by taking a second mortgage or cashing out the equity from their homes. Refinancing their homes to pay down other bills is the single biggest mistake made by families in trouble. *Do not do it!*

If you are in financial trouble, you will probably be steered into a high-cost, subprime mortgage, making any gains illusory. Worst of all, you will be jeopardizing the roof over your family's head. If a mortgage lender gives you a lower rate than a credit card company, it is because the mortgage lender gets something in return—the right to push you into the street, seize your home, and sell it.

If your troubles become bad enough, you can file for bankruptcy to eliminate your high-interest credit card debts and cash advances, but bankruptcy cannot help with a home equity loan or a refinanced mortgage. You must pay the mortgage lender in full—plus all penalties, late fees, and interest—or face foreclosure. The chance to save a few dollars a month on your credit card bills is not worth risking the home you live in.

Remember that creditors who have security interests—a home mortgage company and a car lender, for example—must be paid if the family wants to hold on to these assets. And some debts are never forgiven, no matter what. Taxes, student loans, alimony, and child support must be paid in full, regardless of how long it takes; bankruptcy offers no relief whatsoever to these obligations.

Achieving financial freedom

Many families make a reasonably good income but do not know where the money goes. By making a simple budget, they can see where it all went. Make a record of all expenditures for three months, then identify and eliminate any unnecessary items. Why not set goals for your family? Pay off some debt by a set date. Save up cash to purchase your next car.

Credit cards are one of the major causes of family indebtedness. If you find that you are not paying off the cards in total each month or that you are using them to purchase items that you would not have otherwise purchased, you should destroy your credit cards before they destroy you or your marriage.

Many folks find that they spend less when they use cash for their purchases. When you save up for an item, you are more likely to make sure you get the best deal available when you purchase it.

Watch the small things. Take utilities, for example. Just keeping your thermostat a little higher in summer and a little lower in winter and turning out the lights in rooms not being used can save a significant amount over the course of a year.

Take inventory of all of your possessions, and sell off what you do not absolutely need. Why not collect all this stuff, have a yard sale, and apply the proceeds toward your debt?

But enough about the problems. Let us focus now on what you can do to experience financial freedom. The Bible says, "The rich rules over the poor, and the borrower is servant to the lender" (Proverbs 22:7). (Some Bible translations say "slave" instead of "servant.") No one probably needs to be told that debt is bad. It is almost like telling people who smoke that smoking is harmful. They already know that. What they need is help. What can be done to insulate your family from this unfortunate phenomenon? Is there anything that a family can do to eliminate the embarrassment and stress of unmanageable debt? The resounding answer is *yes!*

If you are out of debt, thank the Lord and those who trained you. If you are in debt, the following outline will help you begin a debt-elimination process that will bring financial freedom to your family.

The plan is simple. The basic premise is a commitment to God to be faithful in returning His holy tithe to access His wisdom and blessing (Proverbs 3; Deuteronomy 28; Malachi 3). No one should honestly expect God's blessing while robbing Him. He is eager to bless those who obey Him.

Three steps

The following three steps were written by Ellen White in 1877 and are found in *Counsels on Stewardship*. I will give her relevant counsel following each step.

1. Declare a moratorium on additional debt. No more credit spending! If you do not borrow money, you cannot get further into debt. "Be determined never to incur another debt. Deny yourself a thousand things rather than run in debt. This has been the curse of your life, getting into debt. Avoid it as you would the smallpox."[10]

2. Make a covenant (a promise or agreement) with God that from this point on, as He blesses, you will pay off your debts as quickly as possible. Set a target date for being debt-free. When God blesses you financially, use the money to reduce your debt, not purchase more things. This step is probably the most critical. When people receive unexpected money, they often spend it. But if you have made a covenant with God, you will then know what to do with the extra money. You will apply it to your debt-reduction plan.

Some time ago, a man came up to me and remarked, "How true

this covenant business is! We received twenty-five hundred dollars that we were not expecting, so I told my wife, 'How did God know that we needed a new riding lawn mower?' Then I promptly went out and bought one. Now I realize that I should have put the money on my debts." "Make a solemn covenant with God that by His blessing you will pay your debts, and then owe no man anything if you live on porridge and bread."[11]

3. Make a list of all of your debts from the largest to the smallest in descending order. For most families, the home mortgage is at the top of the list and a credit card or personal debt is at the bottom. Begin by making at least the minimum payment due on each of your debts on a monthly basis. Next, double up or increase, in any way you can, your payments on the debt at the bottom of the list. You will be pleasantly surprised at how quickly you can eliminate that smallest debt. Then use the money that you were paying on the bottom debt to add to the basic payment on the next debt as you work your way up the list. As you eliminate your smaller high-interest debts, you will free up a surprising amount of money to place on the next higher debts. "Work them off as fast as possible [using your list]. When you can stand forth a free man again, owing no man anything, you will have achieved a great victory."[12] God does not want us to be in debt and will eagerly bless us in unexpected ways. Once the covenant is made, many families find that the debt is reduced faster than they had anticipated.

When you reach the home mortgage at the top of your debt list, you can begin to make additional payments on the principal of your loan, thereby saving considerable interest that you would have had to pay. Of course, you also reduce the length of the loan as well.

By following these three simple steps, many families have become debt-free. You can too! By putting God first, you will receive His wisdom and blessing for managing what He has entrusted to you. By eliminating debt, you are freer to participate in advancing the cause of God and in helping others, thereby storing up treasure in heaven.

1. Gordon Botting, "Life After Debt," *Inside Report*, April 2002, 5, 6, https://www.amazingfacts.org/news-and-features/inside-report/magazine/id/10759/t/life-after-debt.

2. Ellen G. White, *Counsels on Stewardship* (Washington, DC: Review and Herald®, 1940), 249.

3. Botting, "Life After Debt."

4. Botting.

5. Botting.

6. Botting.

7. Botting.

8. Ellen G. White, *Testimonies for the Church*, vol. 5 (Mountain View, CA: Pacific Press®, 1948), 179.

9. Botting, "Life After Debt."

10. White, *Counsels on Stewardship*, 257.

11. White, 257.

12. White, 257.

6

Laying Up Treasure in Heaven

"Do not lay up for yourselves treasures on earth, where moth and rust destroy and where thieves break in and steal; but lay up for yourselves treasures in heaven, where neither moth nor rust destroys and where thieves do not break in and steal. For where your treasure is, there your heart will be also."
—Matthew 6:19–21

There is ample counsel in the Bible and the Spirit of Prophecy regarding the use of our resources, spending them wisely, and keeping them safe. Here is an example:

Many of the people of God are stupefied by the spirit of the world, and are denying their faith by their works. They cultivate a love for money, for houses and lands, until it absorbs the powers of mind and being, and shuts out love for the Creator and for souls for whom Christ died. The god of this world has blinded their eyes; their eternal interests are made secondary; and brain, bone, and muscle are taxed to the utmost to increase their worldly possessions. And all this accumulation of cares and burdens is borne in direct violation of the injunction of Christ, who said, "Lay not up for yourselves treasures upon earth, where moth and rust doth corrupt, and where thieves break through and steal."

They forget that He said also, "Lay up *for yourselves* treasures in heaven;" that in so doing they are working for their own interest. The treasure laid up in heaven is safe; no thief can approach nor moth corrupt it. But their treasure is upon the earth, and their affections are upon their treasure.[1]

All in for God

Many of the Bible's characters demonstrated their deep commitment to God, but that level of commitment is not commonly seen in the lives of Christians today. This deep commitment shows that a person has transformed from having a selfish, me-first attitude to one of total dedication to God. These people regularly store up their treasures in heaven.

As a young man, Moses made a life-changing decision with eternal consequences. The Bible records his decision in Hebrews 11:

> By faith Moses, when he became of age, refused to be called the son of Pharaoh's daughter, choosing rather to suffer affliction with the people of God than to enjoy the passing pleasures of sin, esteeming the reproach of Christ greater riches than the treasures in Egypt; for he looked to the reward.
>
> By faith he forsook Egypt, not fearing the wrath of the king; for he endured as seeing Him who is invisible (verses 24–27).

After the forty years of wilderness wandering, Moses again led the Israelites to the borders of the Promised Land. Since he was not permitted to enter Canaan, he gave the Israelites three farewell presentations—both orally and in writing. Near the beginning of his second presentation, he spoke these words:

> "Hear, O Israel: The LORD our God, the LORD is one! You shall love the LORD your God with all your heart, with all your soul, and with all your strength.
>
> "And these words which I command you today shall be in your heart. You shall teach them diligently to your children, and shall talk of them when you sit in your house, when you walk by the

way, when you lie down, and when you rise up" (Deuteronomy 6:4–7).

The first two verses of this passage (verses 4, 5) have become known as the Shema. These words have been memorized and quoted by the Jewish people as part of their morning devotions for centuries. It is significant to note that Jesus quoted the Shema during His earthly ministry:

Then one of the scribes came, and having heard them reasoning together, perceiving that He had answered them well, asked Him, "Which is the first commandment of all?"

Jesus answered him, "The first of all the commandments is: 'Hear, O Israel, the Lord our God, the Lord is one. And you shall love the Lord your God with all your heart, with all your soul, with all your mind, and with all your strength.' This is the first commandment. And the second, like it, is this: 'You shall love your neighbor as yourself.' There is no other commandment greater than these" (Mark 12:28–31).

The significance of Jesus' description of a committed follower of God is that he loves and trusts God with all his heart, all his soul, all his mind, all his strength, and he loves his neighbor as himself. "All" means *all—everything*. All in! Most of the patriarchs, prophets, judges, and Jesus' disciples had to make total life-changing decisions and go all in to follow the call of God.

Check it out for yourself. There was Noah, who most people thought was crazy—a monomaniac who interrupted his "normal" life, spending 120 years preaching about the coming destruction by a flood of water and building a large boat on dry land. He likely had to draw from his savings to pay the workers and buy the materials to build the ark. And after all that time, money, and effort, he only saved his family. Let us say this another way: he saved his own family. Reward enough! And he is recorded as one of the heroes of faith in Hebrews 11.

We could also mention Abraham, who was apparently living a normal life in his hometown of Ur. He was asked by God to leave all that was dear to him and take a life-changing journey to a foreign land, never to return. It is likely that Abraham had a comfortable home in Ur. But by following God, he spent the rest of his life living in a tent. Why was he willing to make this drastic change? The Bible tells us, "By faith Abraham obeyed when he was called to go out to the place which he would receive as an inheritance. And he went out, not knowing where he was going. By faith he dwelt in the land of promise as in a foreign country, dwelling in tents with Isaac and Jacob, the heirs with him of the same promise; for he waited for the city which has foundations, whose builder and maker is God" (Hebrews 11:8–10). Apparently, the hope of his eternal inheritance was his motivation. He was all in for God. He believed that the city that God was building was way better than his hometown of Ur.

In the New Testament, the life of the apostle Paul demonstrates what it means to be all in for God. Following the Damascus road experience, Paul went from being a strict, legalistic Pharisee and a persecutor of the Christian church to become an itinerant preacher to the Gentiles. He went from a life of relative ease to being whipped, beaten, stoned, shipwrecked, criticized, thirsty, hungry, and finally beheaded. Just before he died, Paul told Timothy, his young protégé, "I have fought the good fight, I have finished the race, I have kept the faith. Finally, there is laid up for me the crown of righteousness, which the Lord, the righteous Judge, will give to me on that Day, and not to me only but also to all who have loved His appearing" (2 Timothy 4:7, 8).

What does it mean to be totally committed to God—to be all in for God? These two short statements give a precise answer.

- "Those who are called to unite with Christ must leave all, in order to follow Him. Old associations must be broken up, plans of life relinquished, earthly hopes surrendered. In toil and tears, in solitude, and through sacrifice, must the seed be sown."[2]
- "Lay all upon His altar—self, property, and all, a living sacrifice. It will take all to enter glory. Lay up for yourselves treasure in heaven, where no thief can approach or rust corrupt. Ye must

be partakers of Christ's sufferings here if ye would be partakers with Him of His glory hereafter."[3]

"For what will it profit a man if he gains the whole world, and loses his own soul? Or what will a man give in exchange for his soul?" (Mark 8:36, 37).

How to store up treasure in heaven

The story of the rich young ruler, recorded in all three synoptic Gospels, is given an entire chapter in *The Desire of Ages*.[4] We are not told the ruler's name, only that he spent a few minutes with Jesus and was never heard from again. He was apparently an upstanding man in every other way, but he chose money over God. "He went away sorrowful, for he had great possessions" (Matthew 19:22). He desired eternal life, but he was not willing to make the sacrifice it required. This story is important because it highlights a way to store up treasure in heaven and also illustrates the strong pull of earthly possessions on our hearts. "Jesus said to him, 'If you want to be perfect, go, sell what you have and give to the poor, and you will have treasure in heaven; and come, follow Me' " (verse 21).

Ellen White makes these points about the story:

Christ's dealing with the young man is presented as an object lesson. God has given us the rule of conduct which every one of His servants must follow. It is obedience to His law, not merely a legal obedience, but an obedience which enters into the life, and is exemplified in the character. God has set His own standard of character for all who would become subjects of His kingdom. Only those who will become co-workers with Christ, only those who will say, Lord, all I have and all I am is Thine, will be acknowledged as sons and daughters of God. All should consider what it means to desire heaven, and yet to turn away because of the conditions laid down.[5]

As Jesus told the rich young ruler and as noted in the following statement, there are two main ways to store up treasure in heaven:

"Every opportunity to help a brother in need, or to aid the cause of God in the spread of the truth, is a pearl that you can send beforehand and deposit in the bank of heaven for safekeeping. . . . Every such opportunity improved adds to your heavenly treasure."[6] "Better than a title to the noblest palace on earth is a title to the mansions our Lord has gone to prepare. And better than all the words of earthly praise will be the Saviour's words to His faithful servants, 'Come, ye blessed of My Father, inherit the kingdom prepared for you from the foundation of the world.' Matthew 25:34."[7]

The treasure principle

Two Bible texts reveal the treasure principle. The first is 1 Timothy 6:6, 7: "Now godliness with contentment is great gain. For we brought nothing into this world, and it is certain we can carry nothing out." When we leave this earth, we will not take any of our possessions with us. The second text is Matthew 6:19, 20: "Do not lay up for yourselves treasures on earth, where moth and rust destroy and where thieves break in and steal; but lay up for yourselves treasures in heaven, where neither moth nor rust destroys and where thieves do not break in and steal." In these two texts, Jesus counsels us to store up treasures in heaven. This is the treasure principle. We cannot take it with us—but we *can* send it on ahead!

As Bible-believing Christians, we have inside information. We know that this world's economy will take a nosedive and never recover. Further, we know that everything that is not sent on ahead will be burned up. And that will reduce its value considerably! This should be a major motivation to store up treasure in heaven. With the treasure principle in mind, Ellen White counseled, "The work of God is to become more extensive, and if His people follow His counsel, there will not be much means in their possession to be consumed in the final conflagration. All will have laid up their treasure where moth and rust cannot corrupt; and the heart will not have a cord to bind it to earth."[8]

Hidden treasure

The shortest of the kingdom parables, recorded in Matthew 13:44, illustrates what it means to understand the value of the gospel and Jesus as our Savior. The parable also demonstrates total commitment and what it means to be all in for God. "Again, the kingdom of heaven is like treasure hidden in a field, which a man found and hid; and for joy over it he goes and sells all that he has and buys that field."

This is a power-packed one-verse parable about a man who finds a valuable treasure. He rents a tract of land from another person to cultivate and raise a crop, and as the man is plowing up the new ground, his ox-drawn plow uncovers a cache of hidden treasure. He stops his oxen, drops to his knees, and with his hands, scrapes back the loose soil. He realizes that a fortune is within his reach. He quickly covers over the cache of treasure and finishes plowing the field so that it is not obvious to others where the buried treasure is located.

In Bible times, it was common for people to hide their treasures in the earth. Thefts and robberies happened regularly. And the land was invaded by foreigners, such as the Philistines, who ransacked their homes and granaries and left them with almost nothing. Hiding their wealth in the earth was considered a safe place. Unfortunately, the owners of the hidden treasures might forget where they hid the treasure, they could die or be killed, or they could be taken captive to a foreign land. Then the treasure, which they took such pains to conceal, would be left to the fortunate person who discovered it.

The man in the parable becomes very excited about what he has found. The treasure captivates him. It becomes the basis of his dreams. He becomes single-minded about it and decides to purchase the field, no matter the cost. It ends up costing him everything, but he makes the sacrificial purchase with joy in his heart. He now sees life through different eyes. His family, friends, and neighbors think he has lost his mind. But he knows what he is doing.

We are told, "This parable illustrates the value of the heavenly treasure, and the effort that should be made to secure it. The finder of the treasure in the field was ready to part with all that he had, ready to put forth untiring labor, in order to secure the hidden riches. So the finder of heavenly treasure will count no labor too great and no sacrifice too dear, in order to gain the treasures of truth."[9] This story echoes the advice found in Jeremiah: "And you will seek Me and find Me, when you search for Me with all your heart" (Jeremiah 29:13).

Cause for concern

"If your thoughts, your plans, your purposes, are all directed toward the accumulation of the things of earth, your anxiety, your study, your interests, will all be centered upon the world. The heavenly attractions will lose their beauty. . . . Your heart will be with your treasure. . . . You will have no time to devote to the study of the Scriptures and to earnest prayer that you may escape the snares of Satan."[10]

Unfortunately, many Christians are storing up treasures on this earth. And what are the consequences? As we have seen, it means an anxious life now and the loss of eternal treasure later. If we are in that group, the nearer we get to our earthly death or the Second Coming, the further we are from our treasures because we have laid them up on Earth. Jesus says, "Turn around. Look the other direction, and face eternity head-on. Lay up for yourselves treasures in heaven." Heeding His advice will move us toward our treasures instead of backing away from them. People who spend their lives backing away from their treasures have reason to despair, but those who spend their lives headed toward their treasures have reason to rejoice. "And for joy over it he goes and sells all that he has and buys that field" (Matthew 13:44).

Remember Lot's wife

Lot entered Sodom a very wealthy man (Genesis 13:5). Around twenty years later, he exited Sodom with nothing but the clothes on his back. His wife left her heart in Sodom and did not fare so well. Hence Jesus' advice: "Remember Lot's wife" (Luke 17:32). When asked about conditions on the earth just before His second coming, He referenced Noah's day and the time of Lot in Sodom. (You can read the entire sad story of Lot and his family in Genesis 18 and 19 and in *Patriarchs and Prophets*.[11])

God, in His love and mercy, personally visited Sodom, accompanied by two angels. He knew of the bad reports from the wicked city but first stopped to see Abraham. The two angels went on to Sodom and tried all night long to get Lot and his family to leave the doomed city. They finally just took Lot, his wife, and two daughters and led them outside the city before returning to their work of destruction.

Then God Himself, who had stayed behind to talk with Abraham, drew near to Lot and commanded, "Escape for your life! Do not look behind you nor stay anywhere in the plain. Escape to the mountains, lest you be destroyed" (Genesis 19:17). When Lot argued with God about going to the mountains, his wife looked back and became a pillar of salt (verse 26).

"Lot trod the plain with unwilling and tardy steps. He had so long associated with evil workers that he could not see his peril until his wife stood on the plain a pillar of salt forever."[12] Why did she look back? She looked back because her heart was in Sodom; her possessions were still in the city, and some of her children were too.

When Jesus said, "Remember Lot's wife," He did so because every person who leaves this world alive will face the same decision as Lot's wife. We all will have friends and family here who may not choose to follow God and stand for Him. We all will have some possessions here that we have worked hard to accumulate. Leaving it all, along with our memories, will not be an easy decision to make. In fact, the only way to make that decision in the future is to choose Jesus in the present. Make the choice now. No person or possession is worth trading for eternal life.

1. Ellen G. White, *Counsels on Stewardship* (Washington, DC: Review and Herald®, 1940), 209; emphasis in the original.

2. Ellen G. White, *Christ's Object Lessons* (Washington DC: Review and Herald®, 1941), 36.

3. Ellen G. White, *The Faith I Live By* (Washington, DC: Review and Herald®, 1958), 359.

4. Ellen G. White, *The Desire of Ages* (Mountain View, CA: Pacific Press®, 1940), 518–523.

5. White, 523.

6. Ellen G. White, *Testimonies for the Church*, vol. 3 (Mountain View, CA: Pacific Press®, 1948), 249.

7. White, *Christ's Object Lessons*, 374.

8. Ellen G. White, *Testimonies for the Church*, vol. 1 (Mountain View, CA: Pacific Press®, 1948), 197.

9. White, *Christ's Object Lessons*, 104.

10. Ellen G. White, *Our High Calling* (Washington, DC: Review and Herald®, 1961), 200.

11. Ellen G. White, *Patriarchs and Prophets* (Mountain View, CA: Pacific Press®, 1958), 156–170.

12. Ellen G. White, "An Important Letter From Sister E. G. White," *Review and Herald*, December 11, 1900, 796 (12).

7

Unto the Least of These

"Then the King will say to those on His right hand, 'Come, you blessed of My Father, inherit the kingdom prepared for you from the foundation of the world: for I was hungry and you gave Me food; I was thirsty and you gave Me drink; I was a stranger and you took Me in; I was naked and you clothed Me; I was sick and you visited Me; I was in prison and you came to Me.'"
—Matthew 25:34–36

When Jesus spoke the words of Matthew 25:34–36, the benefactors asked Him, "When did we see You in this condition?" He answered them, "Assuredly, I say to you, inasmuch as you did it to one of the least of these My brethren, you did it to Me" (verse 40).

Ellen White notes the eternal consequences of this declaration with sobering words:

"When the Son of man shall come in His glory, and all the holy angels with Him, then shall He sit upon the throne of His glory: and before Him shall be gathered all nations: and He shall separate them one from another." [Matthew 25:31, 32.] Thus Christ on the Mount of Olives pictured to His disciples the scene of the great judgment day. And He represented its decision as turning upon one point. When the nations are gathered before Him, there will be but two classes, and their eternal destiny will be determined by what they have done or have neglected to do for Him in the person of the poor and the suffering.[1]

We must understand that as Christians—the sons and daughters of God—we have a responsibility to love and care for God's other children, just as He would. But without God's help and guidance, we face an impossible challenge.

In the world of finance, the rich are getting richer, and the poor are getting poorer. The four hundred richest people in America are all billionaires! Worldwide, there are more than twenty-six hundred billionaires with combined assets of $12.7 trillion.

This group of superrich can be contrasted with the superpoor. Worldwide, there are more than 689 million people that live on two dollars or less per day. For every billionaire, there are 265,000 people on the verge of starvation.

The superrich average around 9.2 percent annual return on their assets, which is much more than what the superpoor earn in their combined total income. The ratio is one million to one. For every dollar earned by the poor, the rich earn one million!

You may know the names of many of the rich. Let me introduce you to the billion superpoor. You will meet them in the villages of Africa and Asia and the highlands of the Andes. They will be delighted to meet you as well, with a hearty smile, a handshake, and offers of food. Alas, their generous offering to you likely means no meal for them that day!

Up to three-fourths of the superpoor are hungry farm families. The rest—many of whom are hungry and newly arrived from the countryside—are in urban slums. Surprisingly, the farmers do not have enough food for themselves, much less to sell to the market. They are caught in a vicious environmental and financial cycle. They plant each year without the benefit of fertilizers and high-yield seeds, which they cannot afford. The result is a harvest yield around one-third of what it should be, and the remaining nutrients in their soils are continually being depleted by each harvest.

The farmers have no collateral, no savings, and no ability to borrow, subprime or otherwise. They cannot bear the risk of even a standard loan, if they could obtain one somehow. In the event of a drought, the farmers would be forced to default on their debt and would lose their land—and, quite possibly, their lives to extreme hunger and disease.

That is the economy of the bottom 689 million—little food, no assets, and meager (if any) cash income. No collateral, no credit, and no fertilizer. And in their villages, no roads, no electricity, no sewage systems, no clinics, and no safe drinking water. But yes, warmth, humanity, hard work, and love for their children. And hope, especially hope, even in the faces of their children dying of malaria for want of one-dollar medicine or a five-dollar bed net.

The causes of poverty

In addition to the subsistence farmers described above, who are caught in a cycle they cannot escape because of limited resources and a lack of education, there are millions of others who, because of circumstances beyond their control, are now counted among the needy of Earth.

Wars are a significant cause of poverty and need. For example, during the civil war in Syria, it has been estimated that more than five million people have fled for their lives. Most of these refugees walked to friendlier countries with only what they could carry on their persons. They left behind their homes and earthly possessions. Many of these people are now living in refugee camps.

Other causes of poverty are natural disasters, such as hurricanes, floods, and fires, which destroy homes and displace people. Frequently, the sickness or death of a family's primary wage earner will change the economic situation of the other family members. Sometimes poverty is caused by alcohol, drug abuse, or gambling. Then, of course, there are those who live in poverty because they are lazy and will not work. The Bible calls the lazy person a sluggard (see Proverbs 19:15).

How do these economic and social realities affect our church and the rest of the world? The reaction is mixed. Many of the middle class and the wealthy desire more money and seem not to notice or care about the plight of others. Fortunately, there are others—from every socioeconomic status—who are putting forth efforts to make a difference in the world.

Unto the Least of These

The poor in the church

On a Sabbath visit to the synagogue in His hometown of Nazareth, Jesus set a standard of ministry for His followers. He was asked to read the scripture lesson and was handed the book of Isaiah. He opened to chapter 61 and read the first two verses:

> "The Spirit of the LORD is upon Me,
> Because He has anointed Me
> To preach the gospel to the poor;
> He has sent Me to heal the brokenhearted,
> To proclaim liberty to the captives
> And recovery of sight to the blind,
> To set at liberty those who are oppressed;
> To proclaim the acceptable year of the LORD."

Then He closed the book, and gave it back to the attendant and sat down. And the eyes of all who were in the synagogue were fixed on Him. And He began to say to them, "Today this Scripture is fulfilled in your hearing" (Luke 4:18–21).

What an announcement! What a challenge! When Moses recorded the laws given by God for His people, special provision was made for the poor among them. "If there is among you a poor man of your brethren, within any of the gates in your land which the LORD your God is giving you, you shall not harden your heart nor shut your hand from your poor brother, but you shall open your hand wide to him and willingly lend him sufficient for his need, whatever he needs. . . . For the poor will never cease from the land; therefore I command you, saying, 'You shall open your hand wide to your brother, to your poor and your needy, in your land' " (Deuteronomy 15:7, 8, 11).

God also told the farmers to leave some of the grain, olives, and grapes for the poor at the time of harvest (Deuteronomy 24:19–21). In the well-known Old Testament story of Ruth, it was through her practice of gleaning that she met Boaz, her future husband.

The early New Testament Christian church faced some serious financial challenges. "Many of these early believers were immediately cut off from family and friends by the zealous bigotry of the Jews, and it was necessary to provide them with food and shelter."[2] The church dealt with this problem by sharing "things in common" (Acts 4:32). Those who had houses and lands sold them and brought the money to the apostles (verses 32–35).

As the church grew rapidly, the financial challenges of the poor continued. It was brought to the attention of the apostles that some of the widows were not receiving their daily provision. It was decided to appoint seven deacons to care for this work (Acts 6:3). "The fact that these brethren had been ordained for the special work of looking after the needs of the poor, did not exclude them from teaching the faith. On the contrary, they were fully qualified to instruct others in the truth, and they engaged in the work with great earnestness and success."[3]

Paul spent considerable time collecting funds to help the needy saints in Jerusalem. His efforts are recorded in 1 Corinthians 16:1–3 and 2 Corinthians 8 and 9. In fact, the delivery of some of these moneys was one of his reasons for his final visit.

Paul counseled the believers, "Therefore, as we have opportunity, let us do good to all, especially to those who are of the household of faith" (Galatians 6:10). We are told,

> In a special sense, Christ has laid upon His church the duty of caring for the needy among its own members. He suffers His poor to be in the borders of every church. They are always to be among us, and He places upon the members of the church a personal responsibility to care for them.
>
> As the members of a true family care for one another, ministering to the sick, supporting the weak, teaching the ignorant, training the inexperienced, so is "the household of faith" to care for its needy and helpless ones.[4]

Interestingly, Ellen White advises the church to exercise wisdom in helping the poor.

> God does not require our brethren to take charge of every poor family that shall embrace this message. If they should do this, the

ministers must cease to enter new fields, for the funds would be exhausted. Many are poor from their own lack of diligence and economy; they know not how to use means aright. If they should be helped, it would hurt them. Some will always be poor. . . . If the church should help such individuals instead of leaving them to rely upon their own resources, it would injure them in the end, for they look to the church and expect to receive help from them and do not practice self-denial and economy when they are well provided for. . . . They are not the Lord's poor.[5]

"When we give to the poor we should consider, 'Am I encouraging prodigality? Am I helping or injuring them?' No man who can earn his own livelihood has a right to depend on others."[6]

The poor in the world
Ellen White's book *Welfare Ministry* gives a balanced cross section of counsel regarding working for the poor. The worthy poor—those poor in the household of faith who would use assistance prudently, those who have become poor through circumstances out of their control, and those who have lost jobs because of accepting the truth—should be cheerfully helped.

But what can we do for the world's superpoor? Obviously, it would take all of the resources of the entire church to even make a small difference. Our primary focus should be the Great Commission (Matthew 28:19, 20) and loudly proclaiming God's last warning messages of Revelation 14:6–12. Then Jesus will come, Revelation 21:4 will become a reality, and poverty will cease to exist.

For the poor outside our household of faith, the counsel is to assist the poor in the neighborhoods where we live and the communities around our churches. But we should become personally involved. "Donations of money cannot take the place of personal ministry. It is right to give our means, and many more should do this; but according to their strength and opportunities, personal service is required of all."[7] When we help the poor, we are demonstrating the love of God for humankind. "Though He was rich, yet for . . . [our sake] He became poor" (2 Corinthians 8:9).

The Isaiah 58 model

Isaiah 58 only has fourteen verses, but it delivers an urgent call for a balanced work for the bodies and souls of others. Apparently, God's people were going through the motions of spirituality, even to the point of getting pleasure from fasting and using sackcloth and ashes. But they felt that God was not with them (verses 1–5). Then God sends this message of guidance:

> "Is this not the fast that I have chosen:
> To loose the bonds of wickedness,
> To undo the heavy burdens,
> To let the oppressed go free,
> And that you break every yoke?
> Is it not to share your bread with the hungry,
> And that you bring to your house the poor who are cast out;
> When you see the naked, that you cover him,
> And not hide yourself from your own flesh?" (verses 6, 7).

If God's people just understood and practiced the ministry outlined in these two verses, God promised great blessings would come to them.

> "Then your light shall break forth like the morning,
> Your healing shall spring forth speedily,
> And your righteousness shall go before you;
> The glory of the LORD shall be your rear guard.
> Then you shall call, and the LORD will answer;
> You shall cry, and He will say, 'Here I am.'
> "If you take away the yoke from your midst,
> The pointing of the finger, and speaking wickedness,
> If you extend your soul to the hungry
> And satisfy the afflicted soul,
> Then your light shall dawn in the darkness,
> And your darkness shall be as the noonday.
> The LORD will guide you continually,
> And satisfy your soul in drought,
> And strengthen your bones;

You shall be like a watered garden,
And like a spring of water, whose waters do not fail" (verses 8–11).

The heaven-sent blessings given to those who minister to others in this manner would include light, healing, protection, righteousness, answered prayers, guidance, and abundant provisions.

The people of God who worked for others would also be involved in spiritual reformation. This spiritual restoration would include proper Sabbath keeping in response to God's blessings.

"Those from among you
Shall build the old waste places;
You shall raise up the foundations of many generations;
And you shall be called the Repairer of the Breach,
The Restorer of Streets to Dwell In.

"If you turn away your foot from the Sabbath,
From doing your pleasure on My holy day,
And call the Sabbath a delight,
The holy day of the Lord honorable,
And shall honor Him, not doing your own ways,
Nor finding your own pleasure,
Nor speaking your own words" (verses 12, 13).

God's capstone promise to His faithful workers was a place in the Holy City (Hebrews 11:8–10).

"Then you shall delight yourself in the Lord;
And I will cause you to ride on the high hills of the earth,
And feed you with the heritage of Jacob your father.
The mouth of the Lord has spoken" (verse 14).

When writing about the message of Isaiah 58, Ellen White notes,

I have no fears of workers who are engaged in the work represented in the fifty-eighth chapter of Isaiah. This chapter is explicit, and is enough to enlighten anyone who wishes to do the will of God. There is plenty of opportunity for everyone to be a blessing to humanity. The third angel's message is not to be given a second place in this work, but is to be one with it. There may be, and there is, a danger of burying up the great principles of truth when doing the work that is right to do. This work is to be to the message what the hand is to the body. The spiritual necessities of the soul are to be kept prominent.[8]

Love as Jesus loved

As recipients of God's extravagant love, it is our honor and privilege to assist those who are poor and disadvantaged. "He who has pity on the poor lends to the LORD, and He will pay back what he has given" (Proverbs 19:17). "Pure and undefiled religion before God and the Father is this: to visit orphans and widows in their trouble, and to keep oneself unspotted from the world" (James 1:27). "Love to man is the earthward manifestation of the love of God. It was to implant this love, to make us children of one family, that the King of glory became one with us. And when His parting words are fulfilled, 'Love one another, as I have loved you' (John 15:12); when we love the world as He has loved it, then for us His mission is accomplished. We are fitted for heaven; for we have heaven in our hearts."[9]

1. Ellen G. White, *The Desire of Ages* (Mountain View, CA: Pacific Press®, 1940), 637.

2. Ellen G. White, *The Acts of the Apostles* (Mountain View, CA: Pacific Press®, 1911), 70.

3. White, 89.

4. Ellen G. White, *The Ministry of Healing* (Mountain View, CA: Pacific Press®, 1942), 201.

5. Ellen G. White, *Testimonies for the Church*, vol. 1 (Mountain View, CA: Pacific Press®, 1948), 272.

6. Ellen G. White, *Welfare Ministry* (Washington, DC: Review and Herald®, 1952), 191.

7. White, 189.

8. White, 33.

9. White, *Desire of Ages*, 641.

8

Planning for Success

Honor the LORD *with your possessions,*
And with the firstfruits of all your increase;
So your barns will be filled with plenty,
And your vats will overflow with new wine.
    —Proverbs 3:9, 10

After the death of Moses, the Lord spoke to Joshua to give him his commission for leading the children of Israel across the Jordan River and into the Land of Promise. God outlined the scope of the Land of Promise and how it was to be divided among the tribes of Israel. Then God told Joshua the secret for his success. "Only be strong and very courageous, that you may observe to do according to all the law which Moses My servant commanded you; do not turn from it to the right hand or to the left, that you may prosper wherever you go. This Book of the Law shall not depart from your mouth, but you shall meditate in it day and night, that you may observe to do according to all that is written in it. For then you will make your way prosperous, and then you will have good success" (Joshua 1:7, 8).

These words from the Lord were a repetition of God's counsel to Moses: "Now it shall come to pass, if you diligently obey the voice of the LORD your God, to observe carefully all His commandments which I command you today, that the LORD your God will set you high above all nations of the earth. And all these blessings shall come upon you and overtake you, because you obey the voice of the LORD your God" (Deuteronomy 28:1, 2). (You may want to take a moment to read the next twelve verses (verses 3–14) and review the amazing blessings God promised to Israel.) These blessings were promised to Joshua and God's people on the condition of obedience, and they were also assured of "good success" (Joshua 1:8) in the conquest of the land of Canaan.

How do we measure success in our lives today? Do the blessings that God promised Moses still apply to God's people at this time in Earth's history?

From a purely secular perspective, success is defined as the accomplishment of one's goals or the attainment of wealth, position, honor, or the like. If wealth and fame are the criteria of success, then professional sports athletes, movie stars, and politicians would be the most successful. But we may all agree that these people are not the happiest folks in the world. Fortunately, God offers a more satisfying definition of success.

John the Baptist

John the Baptist was a miracle child, born to aged parents—Zacharias and Elizabeth, whom the Bible describes as being "well advanced in years" (Luke 1:7). An amazing part of salvation history occurred when Zacharias was taking his turn as a priest, burning incense in the Holy Place of the temple. The angel Gabriel appeared to him with a message from Heaven. (The full story is recorded in Luke 1:5–25.) "Five hundred years before, Gabriel had made known to Daniel the prophetic period which was to extend to the coming of Christ. The knowledge that the end of this period was near had moved Zacharias to pray for the Messiah's advent. Now the very messenger through whom the prophecy was given had come to announce its fulfillment."[1] Gabriel told Zacharias he should name his son John, and then he proceeded to list several aspects of John's life: "He will be great in the sight of the Lord. . . . He will also be filled with the Holy Spirit, even from his mother's womb. . . . He will also go before Him in the spirit and power of Elijah, . . . to make ready a people prepared for the Lord" (verses 15, 17).

By a secular measure, John would not likely be considered a success. He lived a solitary life in the wilderness. He had no formal education, degrees, or status. His clothing was coarse and basic. His public ministry was only three months long. He spent the last months of his life in prison. Then he was beheaded.

But in God's eyes, John the Baptist's life was a success. In fact, concerning John, Jesus told the multitude, "Assuredly, I say to you, among those born of women there has not risen one greater than John the Baptist" (Matthew 11:11).

You may recall that following the apostasy of King Saul, God sent the prophet Samuel to the home of Jesse in Bethlehem to anoint the next king. When Samuel saw the oldest son, who was tall and handsome, he thought surely this must be the one. "But the LORD said to Samuel, 'Do not look at his appearance or at his physical stature, because I have refused him. For the LORD does not see as man sees; for man looks at the outward appearance, but the LORD looks at the heart' " (1 Samuel 16:7). God understands our hearts, our hopes, our fears, and our futures much better than we do. Isaiah put it like this:

"For My thoughts are not your thoughts,
Nor are your ways My ways," says the LORD.
"For as the heavens are higher than the earth,
So are My ways higher than your ways,
And My thoughts than your thoughts" (Isaiah 55:8, 9).

If our ultimate goal is a home in God's eternal kingdom, as it should be, then we must use His standard of success. "Let us remember that we have a heaven to win and a hell to shun."[2] The basic theme of this book is managing for the Master—handling the resources that God has entrusted to us for the benefit of His kingdom until He returns. With this in mind, we should measure success by God's standard and not our own.

Biblical principles for success
As Bible-believing Christians, we live in a scary world. How are we to relate to current conditions? If we choose not to go with the flow,

our lives and financial management reflect a different paradigm. We see the world through eyes different from the secular-minded person.

Jesus told us through His servant John, "Do not love the world or the things in the world. If anyone loves the world, the love of the Father is not in him. For all that is in the world—the lust of the flesh, the lust of the eyes, and the pride of life—is not of the Father but is of the world. And the world is passing away, and the lust of it; but he who does the will of God abides forever" (1 John 2:15–17).

Since God has given us responsibilities, He has also given us principles to follow that will produce ultimate success. From the parable of the talents in Matthew 25:14–30, we learn that God trusts His servants with the management of His assets. "The parable applies to the temporal means which God has entrusted to His people."[3] When the Master returns, He asks for an accounting from His servants. To those who are faithful, He speaks the words "Well done." These words are only spoken to those who manage His assets (their money) in a Christian manner. Accordingly, understanding and practicing the biblical principles of money management are vital to our ultimate success. Here are seven biblical principles that give practical guidance for achieving peace and freedom in your financial world.

Recognize that God is the Owner of everything

Psalm 24:1 proclaims, "The earth is the LORD's, and all its fullness, the world and those who dwell therein." The Lord declares, "If I were hungry, I would not tell you; for the world is Mine, and all its fullness" (Psalm 50:12).

King David, who clearly recognized God's ownership of everything, assembled the leaders of Israel at Jerusalem and told them of his desire to build a house for God. He explained to them that since he was a man of war, God forbade him from building the temple, but the Spirit of God had given him the plans for the building. God told David that his son Solomon would do the actual construction work (1 Chronicles 28).

During the last years of David's life, the leaders and the congregation of Israel contributed willingly to the project. David amassed most of the building materials—gold, silver, bronze, iron, wood, precious stones, and marble slabs—in abundance. In celebration of the people's gifts and God's generous providence, David offered a public prayer of thanksgiving to God. His prayer included these insightful words:

> "Now therefore, our God,
> We thank You
> And praise Your glorious name.
> But who am I, and who are my people,
> That we should be able to offer so willingly as this?
> For all things come from You,
> And of Your own we have given You" (1 Chronicles 29:13, 14).

Even though the king, the leaders, and the people had all contributed by providing the building materials for the temple, David recognized that God was the source of everything and that the people were just returning His own possessions.

As Christians, we understand that we brought nothing into this world and that we will take nothing out of it. While we live on this earth, we are simply managers of what God has entrusted to us. Faithfulness is all that matters. "That which lies at the foundation of business integrity and of true success is the recognition of God's ownership. The Creator of all things, He is the original proprietor. We are His stewards. All that we have is a trust from Him, to be used according to His direction."[4]

When discussing the parable of the talents, recorded in Matthew 25, Ellen White states: "Some think that only a portion of their means is the Lord's. When they have set apart a portion for religious and charitable purposes, they regard the remainder as their own, to be used as they see fit. But in this they [make a] mistake. All we possess is the Lord's, and we are accountable to Him for the use we make of it."[5]

God must have first place in our lives
Right in the heart of Jesus' longest recorded sermon—the Sermon on the Mount—He gives straightforward counsel on Christian management and care of our investments and basic needs (Matthew 6:19–34).

Jesus acknowledges our concerns, stating, "Do not worry, saying, 'What shall we eat?' or 'What shall we drink?' or 'What shall we wear?'. . . But seek first the kingdom of God and His righteousness, and all these things shall be added to you" (verses 31, 33).

God can see our lives from beginning to end. He knows what is best for us and desires that we prosper. This means more than the simplistic question, What would Jesus do? We should ask instead, What is His counsel in this area of my life? In answer to this question, Ellen White offers helpful advice. " 'Honour the Lord with thy substance, and with the firstfruits of all thine increase.' [Proverbs 3:9.] This does not teach that we are to spend our means on ourselves and bring to the Lord the remnant, even though it should be otherwise an honest tithe. Let God's portion be first set apart."[6] Why does God ask us to put Him first in our management? It is not because He is selfish or needs the money. Our God of love says, "Trust Me, and I will bless the rest."

Your purpose in life is to glorify God
Jesus encourages us, saying, "Let your light so shine before men, that they may see your good works and glorify your Father in heaven" (Matthew 5:16). Paul counsels, "Whether you eat or drink, or whatever you do, do all to the glory of God" (1 Corinthians 10:31). This makes perfect sense when we realize for whom we are managing. The worldly seek prosperity in order to spend and accumulate. Christians seek to prosper in order to provide for personal needs and the needs of others and to help advance the cause of God. Christians are God's managers and ambassadors.

Prosperity is having what you need when you need it
From the biblical perspective, prosperity is living with the blessing of God. The book of Psalms begins with these comforting words:

> Blessed is the man
> Who walks not in the counsel of the ungodly,
> Nor stands in the path of sinners,
> Nor sits in the seat of the scornful;
> But his delight is in the law of the LORD,

And in His law he meditates day and night.
He shall be like a tree
Planted by the rivers of water,
That brings forth its fruit in its season,
Whose leaf also shall not wither;
And whatever he does shall prosper (Psalm 1:1–3).

Paul wrote from prison, "And my God shall supply all your need according to His riches in glory by Christ Jesus" (Philippians 4:19).

God has not promised us that if we become Christians, we will become wealthy by the world's standards. But He has promised that if we serve Him, He will provide for our needs, be with us wherever we go, and give us peace in our hearts.

Debt is bad

As we discussed in chapter 5, debt is a form of bondage or slavery to the world (Proverbs 22:7). Jesus said that we are to be a light to the world (Matthew 5:14) and salt that gives flavor to life (verse 13). Unfortunately, when it comes to money, the world is often salting us more than we are salting it. Many Christians find themselves mired in debt, just like the people of the world. If we recognize and follow this single principle to get out and stay out of debt, it would do more than almost anything else to bring peace to our families and prosperity to the cause of God. Debt causes strife in families and stress in individual lives.

Tithe is the minimum testimony of our Christian commitment

As noted in chapter 3, the honest tithe is 10 percent of our income or increase. Only that amount is a faithful tithe. Many great promises are given to those who are faithful with their tithing. When Abram gave a tithe of the spoils of Sodom to Melchizedek (Genesis 14:19, 20), God came to him in a vision immediately following this experience and said, "Do not be afraid, Abram. I am your shield, your exceedingly great reward" (Genesis 15:1). In other words, "Don't worry, I've got your back."

Proverbs 3:5–10 and Malachi 3:8–11 are more examples of God's promises of blessing when we make Him first in our budgets. Failure to recognize and practice tithing removes us from the security of God's wisdom and blessing. What family or person could afford to live their lives without these blessings?

Everyone must give an account to God of his or her money management

There is nothing more certain in Scripture than the fact that we must all face the judgment bar of God (Matthew 25:19; 2 Corinthians 5:10; Revelation 22:12). When settling accounts with those who are faithful, God says, "Well done, good and faithful servant; you were faithful over a few things, I will make you ruler over many things. Enter into the joy of your lord" (Matthew 25:21).

> Those who realize their dependence upon God, will feel that they must be honest with their fellow men, and, above all, they must be honest with God, from whom come all the blessings of life. The evasion of the positive commands of God concerning tithes and offerings, is registered in the books of heaven as robbery toward Him.
>
> No man who is dishonest with God or with his fellow men can truly prosper.[7]

Success statements from the Spirit of Prophecy

"Success in any line demands a definite aim. He who would achieve true success in life must keep steadily in view the aim worthy of his endeavor."[8]

"God only can give true success. Yoked up with Christ, men will become more precious than gold, even than the golden wedge of Ophir."[9]

"There is no branch of legitimate business for which the Bible does not afford an essential preparation. Its principles of diligence, honesty, thrift, temperance, and purity are the secret of true success. These principles, as set forth in the book of Proverbs, constitute a treasury of practical wisdom."[10]

"True success is found in keeping the future life in view. To live for self, to seek your own pleasure, will prove to you an irreparable loss. The Lord has given to man godlike qualities to be used, to be improved—not to diminish, but to increase."[11]

Conclusion

Thus says the LORD:

"Let not the wise man glory in his wisdom,
Let not the mighty man glory in his might,
Nor let the rich man glory in his riches;
But let him who glories glory in this,
That he understands and knows Me,
That I am the LORD, exercising lovingkindness, judgment,
  and righteousness in the earth" (Jeremiah 9:23, 24).

You may never buy a new car, fly an airplane, write a book, or climb Mount Everest, but if you enter heaven with the redeemed of Earth, your life will have been a success. No question about it. On the other hand, you may become wealthy and famous, write a bestseller, and hike the entire Appalachian Trail, but if you miss out on heaven and eternity, your life will have been a failure. And there is no question about that either.

"True success in any line of work is not the result of chance or accident or destiny. It is the outworking of God's providences, the reward of faith and discretion, of virtue and perseverance. Fine mental qualities and a high moral tone are not the result of accident. God gives opportunities; success depends upon the use made of them."[12] My goal as a committed Christian is to use my God-given gifts of talent, health, and treasure carefully. As I do my part, God will surely do His, bringing profit to His kingdom on Earth and His kingdom in heaven.

---

1. Ellen G. White, *The Desire of Ages* (Mountain View, CA: Pacific Press®, 1940), 98.

2. Ellen G. White, *Sermons and Talks*, vol. 2 (Silver Spring, MD: Ellen G. White Estate, 1994), 197.

3. Ellen G. White, *Testimonies for the Church*, vol. 1 (Mountain View, CA: Pacific Press®, 1948), 197.

4. Ellen G. White, *Education* (Mountain View, CA: Pacific Press®, 1952), 137.

5. Ellen G. White, *Christ's Object Lessons* (Mountain View, CA: Review and Herald®, 1941), 351.

6. Ellen G. White, *The Adventist Home* (Nashville, TN: Southern Pub. Assn., 1952), 389.

7. Ellen G. White, *Counsels on Stewardship* (Washington, DC: Review and Herald®, 1940), 77.

8. White, *Education*, 262.

9. Ellen G. White, "Co-workers With Christ," *Review and Herald*, July 30, 1901, 484 (2).

10. White, *Education*, 135.

11. Ellen G. White to Brother Stone, January 6, 1890, in *Letters and Manuscripts*, vol. 6 (Silver Spring, MD: Ellen G. White Estate, n.d.), Letter 23, 1890.

12. Ellen G. White, *Lift Him Up* (Hagerstown, MD: Review and Herald®, 1988), 193.

9

Beware of Covetousness

"Take heed and beware of covetousness, for one's life does not consist in the abundance of the things he possesses."
—Luke 12:15

Luke 12:15 quotes the words of Jesus Himself. In the mind of God, covetousness is a big deal. It is prohibited in the Decalogue's tenth commandment, and the Bible records "the fearful doom" of those who refused to comply.[1] Ellen White notes some biblical examples: "We have before us the fearful doom of Achan, of Judas, of Ananias and Sapphira. Back of all these we have that of Lucifer, the 'son of the morning,' who, coveting a higher state, forfeited forever the brightness and bliss of heaven. And yet, notwithstanding all these warnings, covetousness abounds."[2] Here we might have a little glimpse into the "mystery of iniquity" (2 Thessalonians 2:7, KJV).

Covetousness has been defined as an inordinate desire for wealth or the position or property of another. *Avarice* is a word that is frequently associated with *covetousness* and is defined as insatiable greed for riches. "To live for self is to perish. Covetousness, the desire of benefit for self's sake, cuts off the soul from life. It is the spirit of Satan to get, to draw to self. It is the spirit of Christ to give, to sacrifice self for the good of others."[3]

The tenth commandment states, "Thou shalt not covet thy

neighbour's house, thou shalt not covet thy neighbour's wife, nor his manservant, nor his maidservant, nor his ox, nor his ass, nor any thing that is thy neighbour's" (Exodus 20:17, KJV). From this commandment, it is evident that covetousness can cover a wide range of objects. Covetousness is so spiritually damaging that God chose to warn against it in His great moral law. In the New Testament, Jesus warned against covetousness in the parable of the rich fool. "Take heed and beware of covetousness, for one's life does not consist in the abundance of the things he possesses" (Luke 12:15).

Covetousness is frequently listed with heinous sins that will keep us out of the kingdom of God. "Know ye not that the unrighteous shall not inherit the kingdom of God? Be not deceived: neither fornicators, nor idolaters, nor adulterers, nor effeminate, nor abusers of themselves with mankind, nor thieves, nor covetous, nor drunkards, nor revilers, nor extortioners, shall inherit the kingdom of God" (1 Corinthians 6:9, 10, KJV). In this chapter, we will learn how to detect and overcome covetousness by studying how it ruined the lives of Lucifer and other people on Earth.

The fall of Lucifer
The Bible tells us that Lucifer occupied a high position in heaven:

> "You were the anointed cherub who covers;
> I established you;
> You were on the holy mountain of God;
> You walked back and forth in the midst of fiery stones.
> You were perfect in your ways from the day you were created,
> Till iniquity was found in you. . . .

> "Your heart was lifted up because of your beauty" (Ezekiel 28:14,
> 15, 17).

Additional insights into the mystery of iniquity are found in Isaiah 14:

> "For you [Lucifer] have said in your heart:
> 'I will ascend into heaven,

> I will exalt my throne above the stars of God;
> I will also sit on the mount of the congregation
> On the farthest sides of the north;
> I will ascend above the heights of the clouds,
> I will be like the Most High' " (verses 13, 14).

Ellen White explains,

> Lucifer might have remained in favor with God, beloved and honored by all the angelic host, exercising his noble powers to bless others and to glorify his Maker. . . . Little by little, Lucifer came to indulge a desire for self-exaltation. . . . Instead of seeking to make God supreme in the affections and allegiance of His creatures, it was Lucifer's endeavor to win their service and homage to himself. And coveting the honor which the infinite Father had bestowed upon His Son, this prince of angels aspired to power which it was the prerogative of Christ alone to wield.[4]

The results of Lucifer's covetousness have become what we now call the great controversy. The consequences include the fall of one-third of the heavenly angels, who are now reserved for the fires of hell (see Revelation 12:3, 4: Jude 6, 7). These fallen angels will be joined by billions of the wicked in the final conflagration.

Satan is still tempting humanity with covetousness today. "As Satan sees that his time is short, he leads men on to be more and more selfish and covetous, and then exults as he sees them wrapped up in themselves, close, penurious, and selfish. If the eyes of such could be opened, they would see Satan in hellish triumph, exulting over them and laughing at the folly of those who accept his suggestions and enter his snare."[5]

The fall of man
We do not know how long Adam and Eve lived in the Garden of Eden before that fateful day when they ate of the forbidden fruit. It could have been several years because we are told that Eden was a school.

Angels were their teachers, and they had face-to-face encounters with God. Adam named the animals, and they cared for the Garden. They were living in a beautiful environment with no enemies—nothing to be afraid of. There was only one restriction. "And the LORD God commanded the man, saying, 'Of every tree of the garden you may freely eat; but of the tree of the knowledge of good and evil you shall not eat, for in the day that you eat of it you shall surely die' " (Genesis 2:16, 17).

Lucifer—also known as the devil, Satan, the dragon, and the deceiver—apparently thought to himself, *If I want to tempt Adam and Eve to disobey God, I should try what got me and one-third of the angels. I will use covetousness. I will tell them that God is holding out on them. There is much more for them.*

> Then the serpent said to the woman, "You will not surely die. For God knows that in the day you eat of it your eyes will be opened, and you will be like God, knowing good and evil."
>
> So when the woman saw that the tree was good for food, that it was pleasant to the eyes, and a tree desirable to make one wise, she took of its fruit and ate. She also gave to her husband with her, and he ate (Genesis 3:4–6).

Satan desired to make it appear that this knowledge of good mingled with evil would be a blessing and that in forbidding them to take of the fruit of the tree, God was withholding great good. He urged that it was because of its wonderful properties for imparting wisdom and power that God had forbidden them to taste it, that He was thus seeking to prevent them from reaching a nobler development and finding greater happiness. He declared that he himself had eaten of the forbidden fruit, and as a result had acquired the power of speech; and that if they also would eat of it, they would attain to a more exalted sphere of existence and enter a broader field of knowledge.

While Satan claimed to have received great good by eating of the forbidden tree, he did not let it appear that by transgression he had become an outcast from heaven. Here was falsehood, so concealed under a covering of apparent truth that Eve, infatuated, flattered, beguiled, did not discern the deception. She coveted what God had forbidden; she distrusted His wisdom. She cast away faith, the key of knowledge.[6]

The results of that covetous act are written in history. Adam and Eve were driven out of their Garden home, Cain killed Abel, and the Earth's inhabitants became so wicked and violent that God destroyed all but eight of them in a worldwide flood. Since that time, millions have died in wars and from disease. But worst of all, that sin caused the death of the Son of God, Jesus Christ our Savior.

Balaam, the man with the talking donkey

Israel's forty years of wilderness wandering were coming to an end. While the Israelites were some two million strong, they were unprepared for war. But God helped them defeat Sihon, king of the Amorites, and thus gain control of the land of Gilead. The next and final obstacle between them and the Jordan River was the nation of Bashan. It was a nation of giants. Og, their king, was the largest of them all, and he had sixty fortified cities. Again, God defeated this foe, and Israel was in complete control of the east side of the Jordan River valley. Here they were camped in perfect order for some time while Moses was preparing for the occupation of Canaan.

It was at this time and in this setting that the Moabite king, Balak, could see the large camp of Israel from Mount Peor in the east. Balak consulted with his Midianite neighbors, and they decided to send a group of men to call Balaam, rumored to have supernatural powers, to come and curse Israel. They offered Balaam gold and silver and a position of honor.

> Balaam was once a good man and a prophet of God; but he had apostatized, and had given himself up to covetousness; yet he still professed to be a servant of the Most High. He was not ignorant of God's work in behalf of Israel; and when the messengers announced their errand, he well knew that it was his duty to refuse the rewards of Balak and to dismiss the ambassadors. . . . Balaam

knew that his curse could not harm Israel. God was on their side, and so long as they were true to Him no adverse power of earth or hell could prevail against them. . . . The bribe of costly gifts and prospective exaltation excited his covetousness. He greedily accepted the offered treasures, and then, while professing strict obedience to the will of God, he tried to comply with the desires of Balak. . . .

Balaam "loved the wages of unrighteousness." 2 Peter 2:15. The sin of covetousness, which God declares to be idolatry, had made him a timeserver, and through this one fault Satan gained entire control of him. It was this that caused his ruin.[7]

Balaam refused to go with the men. Hoping to bribe him, they returned a second time with larger gifts and more honors. This time the Lord allowed him to return with the men, with the understanding that he could not curse Israel.

Balaam saddled his donkey and started off to the land of Moab. On the way, the Angel of the Lord met him with a drawn sword. The donkey saw the Angel and ran off the path into a field. The second time the Angel appeared, the donkey spooked and crushed Balaam's foot against a wall. When the donkey saw the Angel a third time, she just lay down on the path. Each time the donkey responded to the Angel, Balaam struck her with his staff. Then, the Bible says that the Lord opened the donkey's mouth, and she asked Balaam, "What have I done to you, that you have struck me these three times?" Balaam said to the donkey, "Because you have abused me. I wish there were a sword in my hand, for now I would kill you!" (Numbers 22:28, 29). Intoxicated with covetousness and consumed with the prospect of riches and honor, he was blinded to the presence of the Angel and mistreated his faithful donkey.

This story does not end well. Balaam only blessed Israel and could not curse God's people. So he was sent back home by Balak. But Balaam, still infatuated with the prospect of wealth, came up with a plan to remove God's blessing from Israel. He shared his plan with Balak:

At Balaam's suggestion, a grand festival in honor of their gods was appointed by the king of Moab, and it was secretly arranged that Balaam should induce the Israelites to attend. He was regarded by them as a prophet of God, and hence had little difficulty in accomplishing his purpose. Great numbers of the people joined him in witnessing the festivities. They ventured upon the forbidden ground, and were entangled in the snare of Satan. Beguiled with music and dancing, and allured by the beauty of heathen vestals, they cast off their fealty to Jehovah. . . .

. . . Those who would have conquered their enemies in battle were overcome by the wiles of heathen women. The people seemed to be infatuated. The rulers and the leading men were among the first to transgress, and so many of the people were guilty that the apostasy became national. "Israel joined himself unto Baalpeor." [Numbers 25:3.] When Moses was aroused to perceive the evil, the plots of their enemies had been so successful that not only were the Israelites participating in the licentious worship at Mount Peor, but the heathen rites were coming to be observed in the camp of Israel. The aged leader was filled with indignation, and the wrath of God was kindled.

Their iniquitous practices did that for Israel which all the enchantments of Balaam could not do—they separated them from God. By swift-coming judgments the people were awakened to the enormity of their sin. A terrible pestilence broke out in the camp, to which tens of thousands speedily fell a prey. God commanded that the leaders in this apostasy be put to death by the magistrates.[8]

As a result of Balaam's covetousness, Israel suffered heavy losses on the border of the Promised Land. Many of the leaders were executed, and twenty-four thousand people died in a plague (Numbers 25:4, 5, 9). Moses sent twelve thousand armed men into the land of the Midianites, and they killed all the men, the five Midianite kings, and many of the women. They found Balaam there and killed him also (Numbers 31:7, 8).

Achan and the beautiful Babylonian garment

It was a time of great rejoicing because Israel had entered the Promised Land. They had crossed the Jordan River at flood stage on dry ground. While the manna had stopped, the Israelites now were eating the produce of Canaan. God's blessings had continued. Jericho, that large, highly fortified city, had been reduced to a heap of rubble.

On the heels of this victory, the people were excited when Joshua sent three thousand men to conquer the little town of Ai. But the army of Israel was routed, and thirty-six of its men were killed. Thirty-six families were mourning the loss of a loved one.

When Joshua heard the sad news, he fell on his face before the ark and remained there the rest of the day. Then God told him that there was an accursed thing in the camp, and he must get up and take care of the problem. Before Jericho fell, Joshua had told the men, "And you, by all means abstain from the accursed things, lest you become accursed when you take of the accursed things, and make the camp of Israel a curse, and trouble it. But all the silver and gold, and vessels of bronze and iron, are consecrated to the LORD; they shall come into the treasury of the LORD" (Joshua 6:18, 19). Most of the men were bringing things back to the Lord's treasury, but Achan stopped by his tent and hid his loot.

Joshua cast lots, and Achan was found to be the guilty party. When questioned, Achan stated, "Indeed I have sinned against the LORD God of Israel, and this is what I have done: When I saw among the spoils a beautiful Babylonian garment, two hundred shekels of silver, and a wedge of gold weighing fifty shekels, I coveted them and took them. And there they are, hidden in the earth in the midst of my tent, with the silver under it" (Joshua 7:20, 21).

Then, according to the Lord's direction, Achan and his entire family were stoned to death, all of their possessions were placed on their bodies, and the pile was burned up (verses 15, 24, 25).

The deadly sin that led to Achan's ruin had its root in covetousness, of all sins one of the most common and the most lightly regarded. While other offenses meet with detection and punishment, how rarely does the violation of the tenth commandment so much as call forth censure. The enormity of this sin, and its terrible results, are the lessons of Achan's history.

Covetousness is an evil of gradual development. Achan had cherished greed of gain until it became a habit, binding him in fetters well-nigh impossible to break. While fostering this evil, he would have been filled with horror at the thought of bringing disaster upon Israel; but his perceptions were deadened by sin, and when temptation came, he fell an easy prey. . . .

. . . For a goodly Babylonish garment, multitudes sacrifice the approval of conscience and their hope of heaven.[9]

Judas

This entire chapter could be devoted to the downfall of Judas. But the following statement gives a summary view:

Satan took advantage of the covetous, selfish disposition of Judas and led him to murmur when Mary poured the costly ointment upon Jesus. Judas looked upon this as a great waste, and declared that the ointment might have been sold and given to the poor. He cared not for the poor, but considered the liberal offering to Jesus extravagant. Judas prized his Lord just enough to sell Him for a few pieces of silver. And I saw that there were some like Judas among those who profess to be waiting for their Lord. Satan controls them, but they know it not.[10]

Judas—quite possibly the most tragic character in Scripture—forfeited his personal friendship with Jesus for a few coins. Yet it was not this solitary act that doomed him; it was the day-to-day decisions to line his own pockets at the expense of the poor that hardened his heart. He pursued the impossible dream of a stake in both kingdoms. To this end, he talked a good line, but it was not to be. The world won him over, and covetousness sealed the deal. It turns out that matters of the heart really matter.

Ananias and Sapphira

Following the great outpouring of the Holy Spirit on the Day of

Pentecost, the church began to grow rapidly. On one occasion, at the temple gate, Peter and John healed a man who had been lame from birth. The Sanhedrin asked Peter and John to give a reason for this man's healing. They replied that it was the power of Christ that restored the crippled man. They were warned and threatened not to teach in the name of Jesus and then released. The disciples met together and prayed for boldness to continue their ministry. God answered their prayer. "And when they had prayed, the place where they were assembled together was shaken; and they were all filled with the Holy Spirit, and they spoke the word of God with boldness" (Acts 4:31).

Many believers began supporting the work more generously, selling their property and donating the proceeds. It is in this setting that we are told about Ananias and Sapphira.

In sharp contrast to the example of benevolence shown by the believers, was the conduct of Ananias and Sapphira, whose experience, traced by the pen of Inspiration, has left a dark stain upon the history of the early church. With others, these professed disciples had shared the privilege of hearing the gospel preached by the apostles. They had been present with other believers when, after the apostles had prayed, "the place was shaken where they were assembled together; and they were all filled with the Holy Ghost." Acts 4:31. Deep conviction had rested upon all present, and under the direct influence of the Spirit of God, Ananias and Sapphira had made a pledge to give to the Lord the proceeds from the sale of certain property.

Afterward, Ananias and Sapphira grieved the Holy Spirit by yielding to feelings of covetousness. They began to regret their promise and soon lost the sweet influence of the blessing that had warmed their hearts with a desire to do large things in behalf of the cause of Christ. They thought they had been too hasty, that they ought to reconsider their decision. They talked the matter over, and decided not to fulfill their pledge. . . . They deliberately decided to sell their property and pretend to give all the proceeds into the general fund, but really to keep a large share for themselves. . . .

But God hates hypocrisy and falsehood. Ananias and Sapphira practiced fraud in their dealing with God; they lied to the Holy Spirit, and their sin was visited with swift and terrible judgment.[11]

Ellen White makes a serious application of this story to those living in our day.

Everyone is to be his own assessor and is left to give as he purposes in his heart. But there are those who are guilty of the same sin as Ananias and Sapphira, thinking that if they withhold a portion of what God claims in the tithing system the brethren will never know it. Thus thought the guilty couple whose example is given us as a warning. God in this case proves that He searches the heart. The motives and purposes of man cannot be hidden from Him. He has left a perpetual warning to Christians of all ages to beware of the sin to which the hearts of men are continually inclined.

Although no visible marks of God's displeasure follow the repetition of the sin of Ananias and Sapphira now, yet the sin is just as heinous in the sight of God and will as surely be visited upon the transgressor in the day of judgment, and many will feel the curse of God even in this life.[12]

How to overcome covetousness
We should ask God to give us the spirit of contentment.

But godliness with contentment is great gain. For we brought nothing into this world, and it is certain we can carry nothing out. And having food and raiment let us be therewith content. But they that will be rich fall into temptation and a snare, and into many foolish and hurtful lusts, which drown men in destruction and perdition. For the love of money is the root of all evil: which while some coveted after, they have erred from the faith, and pierced themselves through with many sorrows. But thou, O man of God, flee these things; and follow after righteousness, godliness, faith, love, patience, meekness (1 Timothy 6:6–11, KJV).

We are told that faithfulness in our tithes and offerings will wean us away from covetousness.

Our Redeemer, who knew man's danger in regard to covetousness, has provided a safeguard against this dreadful evil. He has arranged the plan of salvation so that it begins and ends in benevolence. Christ offered Himself, an infinite sacrifice. This, in and of itself, bears directly against covetousness and exalts benevolence.

Constant, self-denying benevolence is God's remedy for the cankering sins of selfishness and covetousness. God has arranged systematic benevolence to sustain His cause and relieve the necessities of the suffering and needy. He has ordained that giving should become a habit, that it may counteract the dangerous and deceitful sin of covetousness. Continual giving starves covetousness to death. Systematic benevolence is designed in the order of God to tear away treasures from the covetous as fast as they are gained and to consecrate them to the Lord, to whom they belong.[13]

We now can see the wisdom in the words of counsel in 1 John 2:15–17: "Do not love the world or the things in the world. If anyone loves the world, the love of the Father is not in him. For all that is in the world—the lust of the flesh, the lust of the eyes, and the pride of life—is not of the Father but is of the world. And the world is passing away, and the lust of it; but he who does the will of God abides forever."

---

1. Ellen G. White, *Patriarchs and Prophets* (Mountain View, CA: Pacific Press®, 1958), 496.

2. White, 496, 497.

3. Ellen G. White, *Christ's Object Lessons* (Washington, DC: Review and Herald®, 1941), 259.

4. Ellen G. White, *The Great Controversy* (Mountain View, CA: Pacific Press®, 1911), 494.

5. Ellen G. White, *Early Writings* (Washington, DC: Review and Herald®, 1945), 268.

6. Ellen G. White, *Education* (Mountain View, CA: Pacific Press®, 1952), 24.

7. White, *Patriarchs and Prophets*, 439, 440.

8. White, 454, 455.

9. White, 496, 497.

10. White, *Early Writings*, 268.

11. Ellen G. White, *The Acts of the Apostles* (Mountain View, CA: Pacific Press®, 1911), 71, 72.

12. Ellen G. White, *Testimonies for the Church*, vol. 4 (Mountain View, CA: Pacific Press®, 1948), 469, 470.

13. Ellen G. White, *Testimonies for the Church*, vol. 3 (Mountain View, CA: Pacific Press®, 1948), 548.

10

Giving Back

"Blessed are the dead who die in the Lord from now on."
"Yes," says the Spirit, "that they may rest from
their labors, and their works follow them."
        —Revelation 14:13

The three angels' messages of Revelation 14 compose God's last warning to every person on the earth to prepare for Christ's second coming in power and glory. These messages conclude with a description of the faithful saints who are alive and those who have died.

> Here is the patience of the saints; here are those who keep the commandments of God and the faith of Jesus.
> Then I heard a voice from heaven saying to me, "Write: 'Blessed are the dead who die in the Lord from now on.' "
> "Yes," says the Spirit, "that they may rest from their labors, and their works follow them" (Revelation 14:12, 13).

The living saints are obedient to God's commandments and possess the faith of Jesus. The saints who have died are resting from their labors, and "their works follow them." What is meant by the phrase "their works follow them"? Apparently, they are blessed because of their state of living when they pass away.

Giving Back

In a letter to Gilbert Collins, written on January 3, 1902, Ellen White tells him:

> My brother, you may not live long. Have you made your will? We know that you want to be the Lord's right hand, working in cooperation with Him. Even after your life ends, it is your privilege to carry forward His work. Will you please consider this, and return to the Lord His own, that you may know that you have faithfully acted your part, doing what you could? If you do this, when you are called upon to lay off the armor, you will illustrate the words that God instructed John to write: "Blessed are the dead which die in the Lord from henceforth: yea, saith the Spirit, that they may rest from their labors; and their works do follow them." [Revelation 14:13.][1]

According to this interpretation, the works that follow the righteous dead are the good things that are done with the money they return to God when they die. What will be said about us? Can we claim the promise of Revelation 14:13 based on our present estate plans?

For most people, life can be divided into three major phases or segments. The learning years are the first phase—the time in our lives when we learn to speak our native languages, the alphabet, numbers, and colors. Then, our formal education follows, and we learn to get along with others and function in society. The earning years are the second segment of life—we practice our professions, buy our homes, raise our children, establish ourselves in the local church, and develop an even closer relationship with Jesus. The returning years are the third segment of life—our retirement years to the end of our lives.

I refer to the third segment of our lives as the returning years for a reason. We cannot take our possessions with us when we pass away. We are told this in both the Old and New Testaments:

- "For when he dies he shall carry nothing away" (Psalm 49:17).
- "Now godliness with contentment is great gain. For we brought nothing into this world, and it is certain we can carry nothing out" (1 Timothy 6:6, 7).

It comes as a surprise to some folks that after working hard to get an education and then working diligently during the earning years, they must then make plans to give away all their accumulated assets. The distribution of our assets is called estate planning.

The crowning act of stewardship

In the very simplest terms, Christian estate planning recognizes that God is the Owner of everything (Psalm 24:1). Therefore, it is logical to conclude—from a biblical perspective—that when I am finished with what God has entrusted to me, I should return to Him, the rightful Owner, what is left in my estate once the needs of those who depend on me are taken care of.

Many people do not realize that even if they have not created estate plans and executed the appropriate documents to implement their plans, plans have been established and are imposed on them by the state in which they reside. Therefore, everyone, no matter how poor, has an estate plan. The state laws of intestate succession (a person who has died without having made a will) and descent and distribution are applied to the estate. Intestate succession statutes are based on spousal relationships and degrees of consanguinity (blood relationship) to the decedent rather than on the distribution of property according to the intentions and desires of the deceased individual.

Without a properly drafted and endorsed will, a person may not leave any property to a church or charity—even if that person had been a faithful tither and a generous giver during his or her life. The problem with letting the state's laws determine the distribution of one's estate is that if a person dies without a will, the state will assume that only relatives are beneficiaries of an intestate estate. Nothing will be returned to God through a church or charity. A friend who is not a relative will not inherit any property from the deceased either. If no relatives exist, the property reverts to the state. The property is said to escheat to the state. The absence of a will often makes it difficult for family and friends to distribute the assets of the deceased. These concerns show why every adult Christian should have a properly drafted will.

The estate-planning process

When we are honest with ourselves, we must admit that most of us are not excited about getting involved in estate planning—at least the distribution process. It forces us to face difficult issues related to our own mortality, death and taxes, family dynamics, and financial situations. As a result, procrastination is not just a problem; it is the standard practice.

Many people still cling to the old notion that people die shortly after they complete their estate plans. It is not true, of course. What is true is that when we die, we will die prepared and not leave our families and loved ones in the lurch.

Once you have taken inventory of your assets, reviewed your family's needs, and prioritized your charitable interests, you are ready to set up your estate plan. Ellen White wrote two chapters on the important topic of the distribution of our assets: "To [Aged and] Wealthy Parents"* and "Wills and Legacies."† We would do well to study these two chapters for details that will be of interest to us. *Counsels on Stewardship* also has a section discussing estate planning‡ that would be valuable to read at this time.

Two short statements by Ellen White discuss the value of money and give the priorities of its use. "Money has great value, because it can do great good. . . . But money is of no more value than sand, only as it is put to use in providing for the necessities of life, in blessing others, and advancing the cause of Christ."[2] "The very best legacy which parents can leave their children is a knowledge of useful labor and the example of a life characterized by disinterested benevolence. By such a life they show the true value of money, that it is only to be appreciated for the good that it will accomplish in relieving their own wants and the necessities of others, and in advancing the cause of God."[3]

---

* Ellen G. White, *Testimonies for the Church*, vol. 3 (Mountain View, CA: Pacific Press®, 1948), 116–130.

† Ellen G. White, *Testimonies for the Church*, vol. 4 (Mountain View, CA: Pacific Press®, 1948), 476–485.

‡ Ellen G. White, *Counsels on Stewardship* (Washington, DC: Review and Herald®, 1940), 323–335.

I advise a very simple estate-planning process that essentially divides our planning concerns into the three areas recommended earlier:

1. Our needs for the balance of our lives—financial independence
2. The needs of family members—family legacy
3. What is returned to God—spiritual legacy

Financial independence
Financial independence is the foundation of the estate plan. We cannot give everything away because we must keep something in reserve for our own needs. Even those of us who have had to watch our pennies will still have a considerable estate when we finally divest ourselves of the assets that we needed to live on. These assets include the family home, other real estate, automobiles, and personal property, such as furniture, tools, antiques, and collectibles. These items must finally be distributed through our testamentary documents.

We must remember that there are three areas to consider in our estate planning, not just our own interests. It has been stated by some observers that to retire at the age of sixty-five (or earlier) to a life of ease is the devil's alternative to heaven. If a person just quits working to spend his accumulated assets on himself, I would agree. In fact, in one of the few references to retirement in the Bible, Jesus says essentially the same thing.

> "The ground of a certain rich man yielded plentifully. And he thought within himself, saying, 'What shall I do, since I have no room to store my crops?' So he said, 'I will do this: I will pull down my barns and build greater, and there I will store all my crops and my goods. And I will say to my soul, "Soul, you have many goods laid up for many years; take your ease; eat, drink, and be merry." ' But God said to him, 'Fool! This night your soul will be required of you; then whose will those things be which you have provided?'
>
> "So is he who lays up treasure for himself, and is not rich toward God" (Luke 12:16–21).

When commenting on this parable of the rich fool, Ellen White states, "This man's aims were no higher than those of the beasts that perish. He lived as if there were no God, no heaven, no future life; as if everything he possessed were his own, and he owed nothing to God or man."[4] During this stage of life, if we think only of ourselves and ignore the needs of others and the cause of God, we are following the example of the rich fool—and will receive the same reward.

God wants us to care for the needs of others and to responsibly care for ourselves. With this in mind, first review your assets, income, and expenses. Next, set aside a reserve for emergencies and your potential health care needs. Then, you can go on to the next steps of looking at your family's needs and storing up treasures in heaven.

Family legacy
The second area of estate planning is one that involves a lot of emotion. In North America, many people grow up with the notion that when their parents die, they (the children) should be given the parents' assets on an equal basis with other siblings. In this section, I will share what I have come to believe is God's revealed will in regard to children and inheritance. It will be new for many of you, but I believe that you will see that it makes good sense.

Minor children. Minor children are those who are still dependent on their parents for at least part of their food, clothing, shelter, and education. There is little question that minor children should be a major focus of financial attention in estate planning. It should be understood that parents of minor children must make provisions, by way of written documents, for their children's personal needs, education, and guardianship. The goal of Christian parents is to train their children to become independent adults. Then, as the children mature and become independent, parents can update their estate plans to reflect their current situation. (In this chapter, we focus primarily on the retirement planning and distribution of assets that must take place in the lives of retirement-aged parents.)

Grown children. Leaving money or other assets to grown children is another story. It has been an area of estate planning that many financial counselors and others shy away from. They say there is biblical evidence on both sides. For example, Ecclesiastes 2:21 says, "For there is a man whose labor is with wisdom, knowledge, and skill; yet he must leave his heritage [portion] to a man who has not labored for it. This also is vanity and a great evil." And then Proverbs 13:22 says, "A good man leaves an inheritance to his children's children." How is this apparent conflict of verses to be resolved? It is quite simple, actually.

> In Old Testament times, passing on ownership of the land to children and grandchildren was vital. Without it, succeeding generations couldn't do their farming or raise livestock. Many people lived at a subsistence level. Most were too poor to buy land. With no inheritance they could end up enslaved or unable to care for their parents and grandparents, who normally lived on the property with them until they died.
>
> Today in America, however, things are very different. Inheritances are usually windfalls coming to people who live separately from their parents, have their own careers, are financially independent, and already have more than they need.[5]

We have been given practical counsel on how and when to help grown children.

> Parents should exercise the right that God has given them. He entrusted to them the talents He would have them use to His glory. The children were not to become responsible for the talents of the father. While they have sound minds and good judgment, parents should, with prayerful consideration, and with the help of proper counselors who have experience in the truth and a knowledge of the divine will, make disposition of their property. If they have children who are afflicted or are struggling in poverty, and who will make a judicious use of means, they should be considered. But if they have unbelieving children who have abundance of this world, and who are serving the world, they commit a sin against the Master, who has made them His stewards, by placing means in their hands merely because they are their children. God's claims are not to be lightly regarded. . . .

If parents, while they live, would assist their children to help themselves, it would be better than to leave them a large amount at death. Children who are left to rely principally upon their own exertions make better men and women, and are better fitted for practical life than those children who have depended upon their father's estate.[6]

Spiritual legacy
Once our financial independence and children's needs are cared for, we can experience a greater sense of freedom to consider what surplus we have for our spiritual legacy. A motto of the Laymen's Missionary Movement put it very simply: "Not, how much money will I give to God, but how much of God's money will I keep for myself."[7]

When the portion of the estate is identified that can be returned to God, then a decision must be made as to when and how this will be done. Will it be now—inter vivos (while living)—or will it be done with testamentary documents after death? There are many advantages to present giving. An old saying goes, "Do your giving while you're living, then you're knowing where it's going." Ellen White concurs. "That which many propose to defer until they are about to die, if they were Christians indeed they would do while they have a strong hold on life. They would devote themselves and their property to God, and, while acting as His stewards, they would have the satisfaction of doing their duty. By becoming their own executors, they could meet the claims of God themselves, instead of shifting the responsibility upon others."[8]

Options for spiritual legacies
There are hundreds of causes or ministries to support with charitable—spiritual legacy—funds. This is where the family's personal values, beliefs, and interests come into play. If God's holy tithe has already been taken care of, these funds are classified as offerings, and their use is discretionary to the giver. Jesus does give some guidance into the scope of our mission interests: "But you shall receive power when the Holy Spirit has come upon you; and you shall be witnesses to Me in Jerusalem, and in all Judea and Samaria, and to the end of the earth"

(Acts 1:8). You can fill in the names of the cities in your area, but your mission could easily match your community, local church, conference, and world field.

In planning your spiritual legacy, it can be helpful to answer these questions:

- How has your family been blessed over the years?
- How did you come to know the Lord?
- Did you receive a blessing through your educational experience or during a stay in a medical institution?
- Do you appreciate having a church in which to worship?
- Would you like to help pay off your church's mortgage?
- Have you been blessed at summer camp? Have your children been blessed there?
- Would you like to help others learn of the soon coming of Jesus?
- Would you like to help build schools and churches around the world?
- Has your life been blessed by attending evangelistic meetings?
- Would you like to support these organizations? 10/40 window ministries? Adventist World Radio?
- Were you helped by the church during a time of need? Would you like to help others?
- Have you gone on a short-term mission trip? Would you like to see others be able to do so?
- Would you like to support an orphanage or a clinic where HIV/AIDS has brought so much sorrow and pain?

Prayerfully consider these questions and ask God to direct your mind to a worthy cause. You will be an answer to prayer for the ministries you choose to support.

Why a will?
Testamentary documents, such as wills and trusts, are put in place early in the estate-planning process to be a protection against your untimely death and lack of testamentary capacity and to distribute what has not been returned to God before your death.

While a valid will is a good beginning point for an estate plan, the will must be reviewed periodically to assure that it represents the testator's (the person who leaves the will) most recent intentions and will be honored at his or her death. The birth or adoption of children, a divorce or the death of a spouse, a move to another state, or a change in the assets one possesses are common reasons for revising an estate plan. Another significant reason is becoming a Christian and having greater and more specific charitable intent.

Our work for God lives on
For the Christian, the second coming of Christ is the blessed hope. We have all imagined how awesome it will be to see Jesus coming in the clouds of heaven. We are eager to hear the words "Well done." But if we should be laid to rest before He returns, we can have the satisfaction that our estate plan has moved the work forward and helped it continue after we are gone.

---

1. Ellen G. White, *Manuscript Releases*, vol. 4 (Silver Spring, MD: Ellen G. White Estate, 1990), 320.

2. Ellen G. White, *Christ's Object Lessons* (Washington, DC: Review and Herald®, 1941), 351.

3. Ellen G. White, *Testimonies for the Church*, vol. 3 (Mountain View, CA: Pacific Press®, 1948), 399.

4. White, *Christ's Object Lessons*, 257, 258.

5. Randy Alcorn, "Should We Leave Our Children Inheritances?," *Eternal Perspective Ministries* (blog), January 12, 2015, https://www.epm.org/blog/2015/jan/12/children-inheritances.

6. White, *Testimonies*, 3:121–123.

7. George Harvey Trull, *Missionary Methods for Sunday-School Workers*, The "Times" Handbook for Missionary Workers, vol. 1, rev. ed. (Philadelphia: The Sunday School Times Company, 1908), 129.

8. Ellen G. White, *Testimonies for the Church*, vol. 4 (Mountain View, CA: Pacific Press®, 1948), 480.

11

Managing in Tough Times

"Offer to God thanksgiving,
And pay your vows to the Most High.
Call upon Me in the day of trouble;
I will deliver you, and you shall glorify Me."
    —Psalm 50:14, 15

More than one hundred years ago, Ellen White wrote, "The present is a time of overwhelming interest to all living. Rulers and statesmen, men who occupy positions of trust and authority, thinking men and women of all classes, have their attention fixed upon the events taking place about us. They are watching the relations that exist among the nations. They observe the intensity that is taking possession of every earthly element, and they recognize that something great and decisive is about to take place—that the world is on the verge of a stupendous crisis."[1] What would she write now?

Ellen White's perspective on today's world would probably be much like it was during her lifetime. For example, her statement about struggling business operations is just as true today as it was then. "Those who hold the reins of government" "are struggling in vain to place business operations on a more secure basis."[2] The uncertainty of the world's financial situation has many concerned. Rising prices, major supply-chain problems, and trillion-dollar government debts are evident to all. Business leaders, church leaders, and individual families are understandably concerned. What is the appropriate Christian response to all of this?

The Bible principles for success discussed in chapter 8 apply here. Put God first by being faithful with your tithes and offerings and then claim God's promised blessings. Get completely out of debt; liquidate your assets if necessary. Become involved in finishing God's work. Keep your eyes on the prize. Heaven is our goal.

When the clouds of financial uncertainty fill the sky, our natural human tendency is to move into survival mode, cut back on our spending, and conserve our assets. But our thoughts should be on how to do the work of warning the world of an approaching God. "Men are rushing on in the chase for gain and selfish indulgence as if there were no God, no heaven, and no hereafter. In Noah's day the warning of the flood was sent to startle men in their wickedness and call them to repentance. So the message of Christ's soon coming is designed to arouse men from their absorption in worldly things. It is intended to awaken them to a sense of eternal realities, that they may give heed to the invitation to the Lord's table."[3]

The numbering of Israel

When difficult times came to King David, he allowed Satan to tempt him to trust in his own strength and ingenuity. This experience is recorded in 1 Chronicles 21:1–4.

> Now Satan stood up against Israel, and moved David to number Israel. So David said to Joab and to the leaders of the people, "Go, number Israel from Beersheba to Dan, and bring the number of them to me that I may know it."
>
> And Joab answered, "May the LORD make His people a hundred times more than they are. But, my lord the king, are they not all my lord's servants? Why then does my lord require this thing? Why should he be a cause of guilt in Israel?"
>
> Nevertheless the king's word prevailed against Joab. Therefore Joab departed and went throughout all Israel and came to Jerusalem.

Note that it was Satan's idea to count the soldiers. He tempted David to trust in his own strength rather than depend on the providence of God in his defense. Joab, the leader of Israel's army, tried to persuade David not to number Israel, but David demanded that the numbering go forward. As you know from the story, David and Israel suffered through a terrible plague for yielding to Satan's suggestion.

Today, we are faced with a situation similar to David's. What will we do? Will we "number Israel" by counting our money and depending on our own ingenuity to get us through? Or will we do what we can to fortify our homes financially and then trust God to protect and provide? Here is God's counsel:

> Trust in the LORD with all your heart,
> And lean not on your own understanding;
> In all your ways acknowledge Him,
> And He shall direct your paths.
>
> Do not be wise in your own eyes;
> Fear the LORD and depart from evil.
> It will be health to your flesh,
> And strength to your bones.
>
> Honor the LORD with your possessions,
> And with the firstfruits of all your increase;
> So your barns will be filled with plenty,
> And your vats will overflow with new wine (Proverbs 3:5–10).

The battle is the Lord's

An interesting and amazing story is recorded in 2 Chronicles 20, and its principles apply well to our current economic crisis. Our crisis, like the one faced by the kingdom of Judah, has the very real potential to harm God's church on Earth as well as our own individual lives.

Toward the close of Jehoshaphat's reign, the kingdom of Judah was invaded by an army that had the inhabitants of the land trembling. Jehoshaphat, a man of courage and valor, had been strengthening his armies and fortifying his cities. He was well prepared to meet almost

110

any enemy, yet in this crisis, he did not put his confidence in his own strength but in the power of God. He "set himself to seek the Lord, and proclaimed a fast throughout all Judah" (verse 3). In response to the danger, the people gathered together in the temple court, just as Solomon had prayed they would when faced with grave danger. All the men of Judah stood before the Lord with their wives and children. They prayed that God would confuse their enemies so that His name might be glorified. Then the king prayed, "We have no power against this great multitude that is coming against us; nor do we know what to do, but our eyes are upon You" (verse 12).

After the people committed themselves to God in this manner, the Spirit of the Lord came upon a man of God who said, "Do not be afraid nor dismayed because of this great multitude, for the battle is not yours, but God's. . . . You will not need to fight in this battle. Position yourselves, stand still and see the salvation of the Lord" (verses 15, 17).

Early the next morning the king assembled the people with the Levitical choir in the front to sing the praises of God. Then he admonished the people, "Believe in the Lord your God, and you shall be established; believe His prophets, and you shall prosper" (verse 20). Then the choir began to sing, and their enemies destroyed one another, and no one escaped (see verses 23, 24). It took the men of Judah three days to collect the spoils of the battle, and on the fourth day, they returned to Jerusalem, singing as they went.

Lot's wife and the lure of riches
The lure of riches has been a consistent stumbling block for people, even Christians. Many of the New Testament writers warned against the desire for wealth. The following are some prominent references:

- "You cannot serve both God and money" (Matthew 6:24, NIV).
- "The love of money is a root of all kinds of evil" (1 Timothy 6:10).
- "In the last days . . . men will be . . . lovers of money" (2 Timothy 3:1, 2).

Obviously, these passages underscore the perils of our times.

When Jesus was on Earth, the Pharisees asked Him when the kingdom of God would come. Jesus gave them evidence that its coming would not be a secret. Jesus stated, in essence, that no one will have to tell you that He has come the second time. (This experience is recorded in Luke 17.) In fact, He said, if someone says He is over here or over there, do not go see (verse 23)!

Jesus then gave three illustrations to underscore the fact that the Second Coming will be a very big event. The first is a lightning storm with powerful flashes that go from one end of heaven to the other. The second is the experience of the Flood at the time of Noah. Jesus told the Pharisees, "And as it was in the days of Noah, so it will be also in the days of the Son of Man: They ate, they drank, they married wives, they were given in marriage, until the day that Noah entered the ark, and the flood came and destroyed them all" (verses 26, 27). Noah had vainly warned the antediluvians for 120 years. Life was going on normally until, suddenly, the Flood came and destroyed them all at one time.

Jesus continued with a third illustration of what it will be like at His coming. "Likewise as it was also in the days of Lot: They ate, they drank, they bought, they sold, they planted, they built; but on the day that Lot went out of Sodom it rained fire and brimstone from heaven and destroyed them all. Even so will it be in the day when the Son of Man is revealed" (verses 28–30). Just like at the time of the Flood, life in Sodom seemed to be going on quite normally, and then suddenly, the wicked were all destroyed. Jesus concluded His warning to the Pharisees with a terse three-word statement: "Remember Lot's wife" (verse 32). What did He mean by this? What should we do about it?

Lot and his wife accompanied Abram and Sarah when they left Ur.* In Genesis 13:2, Abram is described as "very rich in livestock, in silver, and in gold." Lot also was a rich man (verse 5). In fact, "their possessions were so great that they could not dwell together" (verse 6). Abram suggested that they separate from each other and gave Lot the first choice of the land. Lot chose the beautiful Jordan River valley and

---

* The story of Lot and his wife is recorded, along with the story of Abram, in Genesis 12–19.

"pitched his tent toward Sodom" (verse 12, KJV).

In chapter 14, Lot and his family were living in Sodom when four eastern kings attacked the city and took their goods, their provisions, and all of the able-bodied people to be their slaves. Lot and his family were in the group of captives. When Abram learned of Lot's plight, he decided to attack the kings and rescue his nephew. Through the blessing and providence of God, Abram was successful in rescuing all of the hostages and in recovering all the goods that were taken from Sodom. This is hard to understand, but Lot moved right back into Sodom! Why don't we ever learn?

Lot's next experience is the setting for Christ's short caution: "Remember Lot's wife." Sodom had become very wicked and grossly immoral. This condition was reported to God, and He brought two angels with Him to investigate. Because Abraham was obedient and righteous, God stopped to see him on the way to Sodom. God then told Abraham what He had heard about Sodom and Gomorrah and that He had come to check on the cities. If the reports were true, He would destroy the two cities. Genesis 18 records Abraham's efforts to save Lot and his family from the destruction by bargaining with God. Finally, God agreed that if ten righteous people could be found there, He would not destroy Sodom.

God sent the two angels ahead, and when they entered Sodom, Lot invited them to spend the night as his guests. After supper, which the Bible called "a feast" (Genesis 19:3), but before they retired for the night, a large group of homosexual men surrounded Lot's house and demanded that he send out his guests to them. Lot stepped outside to reason with the immoral crowd—and even offered them his two virgin daughters. They responded by attacking Lot, causing the angels to open the door and rescue him. After smiting the rabble with blindness, the angels revealed who they were and stated that they had been sent to destroy the city that very night. They told Lot to contact family members and warn them to leave immediately. Lot obeyed, but the family members he warned just laughed at him. Apparently, Lot and his wife argued with the angels all night about not wanting to leave their home. "When the morning dawned, the angels urged Lot to hurry, saying, 'Arise, take your wife and your two daughters who are here, lest you be consumed in the punishment of the city.' And while he lingered, the men took hold of his hand, his wife's hand, and the hands of his two daughters, the LORD being merciful to him, and they brought him out and set him outside the city" (verse 15, 16).

Then God, who had stayed behind to talk with Abraham, met Lot outside the city and told him, "Escape for your life! Do not look behind you nor stay anywhere in the plain. Escape to the mountains, lest you be destroyed" (verse 17). Lot told the Lord that he was afraid to go to the mountains and asked to be able to go to the small city of Zoar instead. His request was granted. Unfortunately, Lot's wife looked back and became a pillar of salt. Why did she look back? We are told that she looked back because her heart was still in Sodom, her possessions were still in Sodom, and some of her children were still in Sodom.[4]

When Jesus spoke the words "Remember Lot's wife," it was in the context of being ready for the Second Coming. This sad story tells us that no person or possession is worth trading for eternal life. Every person who leaves this world alive will have made the same decision that Lot's wife faced. Will we decide to stay with our stuff or forsake all and go all in for Jesus?

The devil's last big temptation

John makes it very clear that Satan's final and most serious temptation to God's people will be a financial embargo. All their assets will be frozen. They will not be able to buy or sell and will even face a death decree. "In the last great conflict of the controversy with Satan those who are loyal to God will see every earthly support cut off. Because they refuse to break His law in obedience to earthly powers, they will be forbidden to buy or sell. It will finally be decreed that they shall be put to death. See Revelation 13:11-17. But to the obedient is given the promise, 'He shall dwell on high: his place of defense shall be the munitions of rocks: bread shall be given him; his waters shall be sure.' Isaiah 33:16."[5]

Ellen White was given a view of one of the devil's workers' meetings, and it is obvious that he knows that money will be a major factor in the end-time scenario.

As the people of God approach the perils of the last days, Satan holds earnest consultation with his angels as to the most successful plan of overthrowing their faith. . . .

[The great deceiver says,] "Go, make the possessors of lands and money drunk with the cares of this life. Present the world before them in its most attractive light, that they may lay up their treasure here and fix their affections upon earthly things. We must do our utmost to prevent those who labor in God's cause from obtaining means to use against us. Keep the money in our own ranks. The more means they obtain, the more they will injure our kingdom by taking from us our subjects. Make them care more for money than for the upbuilding of Christ's kingdom and the spread of the truths we hate, and we need not fear their influence; for we know that every selfish, covetous person will fall under our power, and will finally be separated from God's people."[6]

The devil knows that if he can keep us focused on money, it will separate us from God and eternal life. God's strategy is to allow poverty to come on the world so that men will trust in Him rather than their money. Here is what we can expect. "Poverty is coming upon this world, and there will be a time of trouble such as never was since there was a nation."[7] And she writes even more pointedly: "The very means that" are "now so sparingly invested in the cause of God, and that" are "selfishly retained, will in a little while be cast with all idols to the moles and to the bats. Money will soon depreciate in value very suddenly when the reality of eternal scenes opens to the senses of man."[8]

What do genuine Christians do in response to a financial crisis? Do they hunker down in survival mode? No, in fact, just the opposite is true. "In the last extremity, before this work shall close, thousands will be cheerfully laid upon the altar. Men and women will feel it a blessed privilege to share in the work of preparing souls to stand in the great day of God, and they will give hundreds as readily as dollars are given now."[9] Bible-believing Christians know that everything on this earth will be burned up someday soon—at the second coming of Jesus (2 Peter 3:10). They wisely invest their money in God's cause so it will do some good and escape the conflagration. "The work of God is to become more extensive, and if His people follow His counsel, there will not be much means in their possession to be consumed in the final conflagration. All will have laid up their treasure where moth and rust cannot corrupt; and the heart will not have a cord to bind it to earth."[10]

The financial stresses of our economy could be greatly reduced or eliminated by learning and practicing the Bible's principles. God's counsel has been given to us for our best good. In a reflective moment, David looked back on his life and gladly testified, "I have been young, and now am old; yet I have not seen the righteous forsaken, nor his descendants begging bread" (Psalm 37:25). Surely, each of us can likewise see God's hand of blessing in our own lives.

1. Ellen G. White, *Prophets and Kings* (Mountain View, CA: Pacific Press®, 1917), 537.

2. Ellen G. White, *Testimonies for the Church*, vol. 9 (Mountain View, CA: Pacific Press®, 1948), 13.

3. Ellen G. White, *Christ's Object Lessons* (Washington, DC: Review and Herald®, 1941), 228.

4. Ellen G. White, *Patriarchs and Prophets* (Mountain View, CA: Pacific Press®, 1958), 160, 161.

5. Ellen G. White, *The Desire of Ages* (Mountain View, CA: Pacific Press®, 1940), 121, 122.

6. Ellen G. White, *Testimonies to Ministers and Gospel Workers* (Mountain View, CA: Pacific Press®, 1944), 472–474.

7. Ellen G. White, *Evangelism* (Washington, DC: Review and Herald®, 1946), 240, 241.

8. White, 63.

9. Ellen G. White, *Counsels on Stewardship* (Washington, DC: Review and Herald®, 1940), 40.

10. White, 60.

12

Rewards of Faithfulness

But as it is written:
"Eye has not seen, nor ear heard,
Nor have entered into the heart of man
The things which God has prepared for those who love Him."
   —1 Corinthians 2:9

A *reward* is generally defined as something given or received in return for service, merit, or hardship. From an earthly perspective, rewards are offered as incentives or motivations to do something. People offer rewards to anyone who will find their lost pets. In the travel industry, airlines and hotels offer rewards for patronizing their businesses. These offers get people involved in the hope of gaining rewards. But these rewards are insignificant compared to those offered in God's Word. God's promised rewards offer a lifetime of blessings and eternal life. The nature of divine rewards is not often discussed, but the concept is God's idea.

Thinking about, contemplating, and claiming God's promised rewards is not selfishness on our part. These promises motivated Abraham, Moses, and Paul to go all in for God. The following amazing statement about rewards was included by Ellen White in the last chapter of *The Great Controversy.*

A fear of making the future inheritance seem too material has led many to spiritualize away the very truths which lead us to look upon it as our home. Christ assured His disciples that He went to prepare mansions for them in the Father's house. Those who accept the teachings of God's word will not be wholly ignorant concerning the heavenly abode. And yet, "eye hath not seen, nor ear heard, neither have entered into the heart of man, the things which God hath prepared for them that love Him." 1 Corinthians 2:9. Human language is inadequate to describe the reward of the righteous. It will be known only to those who behold it. No finite mind can comprehend the glory of the Paradise of God.

In the Bible the inheritance of the saved is called "a country." Hebrews 11:14-16. There the heavenly Shepherd leads His flock to fountains of living waters. The tree of life yields its fruit every month, and the leaves of the tree are for the service of the nations. There are ever-flowing streams, clear as crystal, and beside them waving trees cast their shadows upon the paths prepared for the ransomed of the Lord. There the wide-spreading plains swell into hills of beauty, and the mountains of God rear their lofty summits. On those peaceful plains, beside those living streams, God's people, so long pilgrims and wanderers, shall find a home.[1]

In Hebrews 11, the famous faith chapter, Paul states, "Without faith it is impossible to please Him, for he who comes to God must believe that He is, and that He is a rewarder of those who diligently seek Him" (verse 6). After discussing the faith of Abel, Enoch, Noah, and Abraham and Sarah, Paul notes, "These all died in faith, not having received the promises, but having seen them afar off were assured of them, embraced them and confessed that they were strangers and pilgrims on the earth" (verse 13). In these verses, it is clear that a faith that is pleasing to God includes both faith in Him as the Savior and belief that He rewards those who diligently seek Him.

The Bible teaches that we are saved by grace alone when we exercise faith in the merits of Christ on our behalf. Jesus also taught that there was a reward for the righteous. He stated, "For the Son of Man will come in the glory of His Father with His angels, and then He will reward each according to his works" (Matthew 16:27). And in the great apocalyptic book of Revelation—the capstone of the entire Bible—Jesus concludes His revelation to John by saying, "And behold, I am coming quickly, and My reward is with Me, to give every one according to his work" (Revelation 22:12).

Life's big decision

Ultimately, every person has to make a big decision—the biggest in life—with eternal consequences. In a December 1897 issue of the *Review and Herald*, Ellen White wrote an article, titled "Christian Liberality," in which she contrasted the rich young ruler and Moses. Then she notes that each of us must make a similar decision:

> To a youthful ruler who inquired of him, "Good Master, what shall I do to inherit eternal life?" Jesus answered, "Sell all that thou hast, and distribute unto the poor, and thou shalt have treasure in heaven: and come, follow me." This was not a hard requirement; for the ruler was not handling his own property. His goods had been entrusted to him by the Lord. The choice was left with him; he must decide for himself. Did he accept the eternal treasure? or did he decide to gratify his desire for earthly treasure, and in so doing, refuse the eternal riches?—When he heard Christ's words, "he went away sorrowful: for he had great possessions." He chose the earthly good, and lost the eternal weight of glory.
>
> Individually, we are tried as was the young ruler. God tests us to see if, as stewards, we can safely be trusted with the eternal riches. Shall we do as the ruler did—fasten our grasp upon the treasures lent us by God, choosing that which appears most agreeable to the natural heart, and refusing to use our possessions as God plainly states he expects us to? or shall we take up our cross, and follow our Saviour in the path of self-denial? . . .
>
> Moses was called upon to choose between the world and God. Two conflicting objects were placed before him. The treasures of Egypt, the honor of a temporal crown, and all the worldly benefits involved in this choice, were presented by the prince of this world. The opposite side was presented by the Prince of Light,

the world's Redeemer. He held out the recompense of reward, the unsearchable riches of Christ, and showed also the path of affliction, self-denial, and self-sacrifice, that must be traveled by all who gain this reward.

The decision was left with Moses. As a free moral agent he was at liberty to choose. All heaven was interested in the matter. What would be his choice?—obedience to God, with the eternal recompense of reward, or obedience to that most agreeable to his own will? "By faith Moses, when he was come to years, refused to be called the son of Pharaoh's daughter; choosing rather to suffer affliction with the people of God, than to enjoy the pleasures of sin for a season; esteeming the reproach of Christ greater riches than the treasures in Egypt: for he had respect unto the recompense of the reward."[2]

Talk about delayed gratification, wisdom, and foresight! Moses made the decision to be a part of God's people, knowing he would face suffering and hardship rather than enjoying a life of wealth and ease as a ruler in Egypt. Why would anyone ever make such a choice? The reason he gave was that "he had respect unto the recompense of the reward" (Hebrews 11:26, KJV). The bottom line is that the rich young ruler clung to his earthly possessions and lost his eternal reward. Moses, on the other hand, laid aside earthly riches for his reward in heaven. His wisdom is reflected in the decision of the man who found the treasure hidden in a field: "For joy over it he goes and sells all that he has and buys that field" (Matthew 13:44). What he gave up was nothing compared to what he gained! He was happy to make the trade.

Rewards now and then
When the rich young ruler left Jesus and the disciples, he went away sorrowful because, to him, the cost of eternal life was too much. Jesus told the disciples that it was hard for those who have riches to enter the kingdom of God. They asked, "Who then can be saved?" (Luke 18:26).

Then Peter said, "See, we have left all and followed You."
So He said to them, "Assuredly, I say to you, there is no one

who has left house or parents or brothers or wife or children, for the sake of the kingdom of God, who shall not receive many times more in this present time, and in the age to come eternal life" (verses 28–30).

So, for Christ's followers, there are rewards now and in eternity.

The Bible records many present-day rewards. There is peace (Isaiah 26:3; Psalm 119:165), personal happiness, less stress, God's protection, improved quality of one's family life, more stability in one's marriage, and a higher level of success in one's career. We can add to that the joy of being in covenant relation with God, the satisfaction of supporting the work of God, and the blessed hope of the second coming of Jesus. Of course, there are many more rewards, and we should often count our blessings.

Jesus concludes the Beatitudes, which open His sermon on the mount, with these words: "Blessed are you when they revile and persecute you, and say all kinds of evil against you falsely for My sake. Rejoice and be exceedingly glad, for great is your reward in heaven, for so they persecuted the prophets who were before you" (Matthew 5:11, 12). Bible prophecy informs us that the last generation on Earth before the second coming of Christ will go through a time of trouble that will be worse than anything ever experienced before (Daniel 12:1). What will keep people buoyed up through this period? It is the knowledge that God has plans for us that are beyond our ability to comprehend.

Paul also saw beyond the shipwrecks, the beatings, and the imprisonments. His hope of a reward in heaven is evident throughout his writings. As an encouragement to others, he wrote, "Therefore, my beloved brethren, be steadfast, immovable, always abounding in the work of the Lord, knowing that your labor is not in vain in the Lord" (1 Corinthians 15:58). Earlier in this same letter, he told the believers in Corinth, "Each one will receive his own reward according to his own labor" (1 Corinthians 3:8). Paul was excited about God's plans for the faithful. He apparently took comfort in his afflictions from the promises in the book of Isaiah regarding heaven and the new earth. He wrote,

But as it is written:

"Eye has not seen, nor ear heard,
Nor have entered into the heart of man
The things which God has prepared for those who love Him"
(1 Corinthians 2:9).

And so, he was committed: "I press toward the goal for the prize of the upward call of God in Christ Jesus" (Philippians 3:14).

What about the treasure in heaven?
"Do not lay up for yourselves treasures on earth, where moth and rust destroy and where thieves break in and steal; but lay up for yourselves treasures in heaven, where neither moth nor rust destroys and where thieves do not break in and steal" (Matthew 6:19, 20).

Christ entreats, "Lay up for yourselves treasures in heaven." This work of transferring your possessions to the world above, is worthy of all your best energies. It is of the highest importance, and involves your eternal interests. That which you bestow in the cause of God is not lost. All that is given for the salvation of souls and the glory of God, is invested in the most successful enterprise in this life and in the life to come. Your talents of gold and silver, if given to the exchangers, are gaining continually in value, which will be registered to your account in the kingdom of heaven. You are to be the recipients of the eternal wealth that has increased in the hands of the exchangers. In giving to the work of God, you are laying up for yourselves treasures in heaven. All that you lay up above is secure from disaster and loss, and is increasing to an eternal, an enduring substance.[3]

From the statement above and many others, it is clear that we all have an account in heaven. There is a ledger there where God keeps a record. The parable of the talents gives an insight into this fact: "For the kingdom of heaven is like a man traveling to a far country, who called his own servants and delivered his goods to them. . . . After a long time the lord of those servants came and settled accounts with them" (Matthew 25:14, 19).

Before we review some amazing statements about the interest rates in the bank of heaven, the safety of the deposits there, and the final utilization of the assets, we must first understand that the primary reward is eternal life with Jesus and the angels—a life with no sorrow, no pain, no tears, and no death. The following statement points out that our reward also includes the joy of seeing souls redeemed:

> When Christ's followers give back to the Lord His own, they are accumulating treasure which will be given to them when they shall hear the words, "Well done, good and faithful servant; . . . enter thou into the joy of thy Lord." "Who for the joy that was set before Him endured the cross, despising the shame, and is set down at the right hand of the throne of God." Matthew 25:23; Hebrews 12:2. The joy of seeing souls redeemed, souls eternally saved, is the reward of all that put their feet in the footprints of Him who said, "Follow Me."[4]

Heavenly investment risk

When we invest on Earth, there is always concern about risk. We talk about relative risk where interest rates are concerned. We know that the promise of a high interest rate is always accompanied by higher risk. But what about the investments that are stored in heaven? We have found some amazing answers. "Those who really feel an interest in the cause of God, and are willing to venture something for its advancement, will find it a sure and safe investment. Some will have a hundredfold in this life, and in the world to come life everlasting. But all will not receive their hundredfold in this life, because they cannot bear it. If entrusted with much, they would become unwise stewards. The Lord withholds it for their good; but their treasure in heaven will be secure. How much better is such an investment as this!"[5]

We can all imagine scenarios in which our temporal security could be lost in an instant: the economy, acts of terrorism, or natural disasters. In fact, we see them in the daily news. People who cling to their earthly treasures will eventually lose everything. But those who are smart will transfer their assets to their new home in heaven. "Everything that is laid up upon earth may be swept away in a moment; but nothing can disturb the treasure that is laid up in heaven."[6]

There is always the temptation to think, *If I can just make it big on this investment, then I will be generous with the cause of God.* Unfortunately, the big return always seems just one investment deal away. Ellen White once wrote to a man who had lost a great deal of money in earthly investments: "The enterprise of securing eternal life did not awaken your interest. Here you could have expended means, and run no risks, met no disappointments, and in the end would have received immense profits. Here you could have invested in the never-failing bank of heaven. Here you could have bestowed your treasures where no thief approacheth nor rust corrupteth. This enterprise is eternal and is as much nobler than any earthly enterprise as the heavens are higher than the earth."[7] She made a follow-up statement regarding the bank of heaven with these words: "Put your money in the bank of heaven. Thus invested, it will yield an infinitely higher rate of interest than if placed in the banks of this world."[8] God's reward to His faithful people is unique and, like many spiritual things, may be beyond our finite understanding. We know that the gift of God is eternal life, but apparently, there is even more. Consider this sentence: "The Lord has a great work to be done, and He will bequeath the most in the future life to those who do the most faithful, willing service in the present life."[9]

But do not confuse the reward with merit. The only merit we ever have is that of Jesus' merit on our behalf. In one of her morning devotionals to the ministers assembled for the General Conference session held in Battle Creek, Michigan, in November 1883, Ellen White stated,

> We shall none of us be saved for our own merits; the rewards of eternity are purchased by Christ, and in no case merited by man; yet ministers should remember that every man will receive according as his works have been. The trials of the great assize will proceed most accurately on the basis of works, and our listlessness

and want of zeal will tell on its decisions. The parable of the talents illustrates this subject. One man becomes ruler over ten cities, another over five, another over two. Each receives in exact proportion to his work—to the improvement he has made on the talents lent him of God; and it is the privilege of each to strive for the highest recompense.[10]

"That which we give to the cause of God becomes our own forever. Says Christ, 'Lay up for *yourselves* treasures in heaven.' These alone, of all that we possess, are really ours. All that we lay up on earth, we must leave at last. It is only what we give for Christ that we can take with us into the eternal world."[11]

To put our reward in its proper place, we must remember that it should not be our primary motive for obedience. Our obedience is a "service and allegiance of love."[12] But when commenting on the story Jesus told of the laborers who worked different hours of the day and each received a "penny," Ellen White notes, "In a subordinate sense we should all have respect unto the recompense of the reward. But while we appreciate the promise of blessing, we should have perfect confidence in Jesus Christ, believing that He will do right, and give us reward according as our works have been. The gift of God is eternal life, but Jesus would have us not so anxious concerning rewards, as that we may do the will of God because it is right to do it, irrespective of all gain."[13]

So let us keep our eyes on the prize. Our hearts will be where our treasure is. The things of this earth, which are soon to be burned up, "will grow strangely dim in the light of His glory and grace."[14] Then, as each day passes, as we near the Second Coming or the end of our lives, instead of thinking about leaving our treasures behind, we can think of our treasures in heaven and realize that we are moving closer to them. "Your thoughts will be fixed upon the great rewards of eternity. All your plans will be made in reference to the future, immortal life. You will be drawn toward your treasure. You will not study your worldly interest; but in all your pursuits the silent inquiry will be, 'Lord, what wilt Thou have me to do?' "[15]

We pray that God will sustain and bless you and your family as you seek His will in this important area of your life. May we all be in the group that hears from the lips of Jesus, "Well done, good and faithful servant. . . . Enter into the joy of your lord" (Matthew 25:21).

1. Ellen G. White, *The Great Controversy* (Mountain View, CA: Pacific Press®, 1911), 674, 675.

2. Ellen G. White, "Christian Liberality," *Review and Herald*, December 14, 1897, 758 (1).

3. Ellen G. White, *Counsels on Stewardship* (Washington, DC: Review and Herald®, 1940), 342.

4. Ellen G. White, *The Desire of Ages* (Mountain View, CA: Pacific Press®, 1940), 523.

5. White, *Counsels on Stewardship*, 232, 233.

6. Ellen G. White, *Our High Calling* (Washington, DC: Review and Herald®, 1961), 195.

7. Ellen G. White, *Testimonies for the Church*, vol. 2 (Mountain View, CA: Pacific Press®, 1948), 280.

8. Ellen G. White, "An Appeal for the Southern Work," *Review and Herald*, May 27, 1902, 21.

9. Ellen G. White, *Christ's Object Lessons* (Washington, DC: Review and Herald®, 1941), 330.

10. Ellen G. White, *Gospel Workers* (Washington, DC: Review and Herald®, 1915), 450.

11. Ellen G. White, "Our Missions in Europe," *Review and Herald*, December 6, 1887, 754 (2); emphasis in the original.

12. Ellen G. White, *Steps to Christ* (Nampa, ID: Pacific Press®, 1999), 60.

13. White, *Counsels on Stewardship*, 339.

14. Helen H. Lemmel, "Turn Your Eyes Upon Jesus," (John M. Moore/ Singspiration[ASCAP], 1952).

15. White, *Counsels on Stewardship*, 343.